THE NILE CAMPAIGN

ILLUSTRATED SOURCES IN HISTORY

THE NILE

NELSON AND NAPOLEON IN EGYPT
CHRISTOPHER LLOYD

DAVID & CHARLES : NEWTON ABBOT

CAMPAIGN

BARNES & NOBLE BOOKS: NEW YORK
(a division of Harper & Row Publishers, Inc.)

This edition first published in 1973
in Great Britain by
David & Charles (Holdings) Limited
Newton Abbot   Devon
in the U.S.A. by
Harper & Row Publishers, Inc.
Barnes & Noble Import Division
0 7153 5449 3 (*Great Britain*)
06 484337 2 (*United States*)

Set in 10 on 12pt Plantin
by C. E. Dawkins (Typesetters) Limited,
London SE1
and printed in Great Britain
by Clarke Doble & Brendon Limited,
Plymouth

CONTENTS

Introduction   7

1   The Capture of Malta (1798)   10

2   The Battle of the Nile (1798)   25

3   The Conquest of Egypt (1798-9)   56

4   The Syrian Campaign (1799)   74

5   The Siege of Malta (1800)   96

6   The Defeat of the French Army (1801)   103

List of Sources   118

Acknowledgements of Illustrations   120

INTRODUCTION

The Nile Campaign includes the story of the capture of Malta by Bonaparte (as Napoleon then called himself) on his way to invade Egypt in 1798, the conquest of that country, and the defeat of the French fleet by Nelson at the Battle of the Nile. This disaster compelled Bonaparte to march through Syria, where he was checked by Sir Sidney Smith's gallant defence of Acre. On his return to Egypt, he himself escaped back to France, leaving General Kléber in command of an army which was ultimately defeated near Alexandria in 1801 by Sir Ralph Abercromby. During the intervening years, Malta was besieged by the ships of Nelson's fleet and when the French garrison surrendered the island became the base for subsequent British influence in the Mediterranean.

The events of those three years, which are described in these pages in the words of eye-witnesses, present many facets of interest. It is not only a military and a naval story, though in this respect it is a classical instance of the conflict between sea and land power, in which the forces engaged were commanded by two of the most brilliant exponents of the art of war—Napoleon and Nelson. It is also a perfect illustration of the character of these two great captains of war. Both were young men at the height of their powers as organisers of victory and leaders of men. Nelson's small Mediterranean fleet under the command of his Band of Brothers was the finest naval fighting force in the age of sail, while the French army, fresh from its brilliant victories in Italy, numbered among its generals—Berthier, Junot, Lannes, Marmont, Kléber—the most distinguished commanders alive, six of whom became marshals in the Napoleonic Empire.

It is, however, Napoleon's genius as a young man which compels the highest admiration. The audacity of his plans to conquer Egypt and develop the country as a French colony, as well as the technical ability of organising and leading such an army to victory, is almost unparalleled. At that period of his life the boundless self-confidence which his belief in his 'star' gave him was only equalled by his extraordinary good luck in evading Nelson's ships, both on the outward voyage and on his humiliating return to France after he had abandoned his army.

But the expedition to Egypt was never intended to be a purely military affair. The versatility of Bonaparte's interests as soldier, politician, legislator and patron of science was never better displayed than during those momentous years. His aim was to found a colony after defeating the Mamelukes, who ruled Egypt under the nominal suzerainty of the Sultan of the Ottoman Empire, and to discover the remains of a civilisation which was almost unknown at that time. He had recently been elected to the Mathematical Section of the National Institute, as the French Academy was now called. He was nearly as proud of his honour as he was of his victories in Italy and he was determined to show that he was something more than a successful general. Five hundred *savants* were therefore included in the expedition, under the leadership of Gaspard Monge. They included some of the most distinguished men of science then alive, as well as nineteen civil engineers and sixteen surveyors and cartographers. When the results of their labours ultimately reached an international public after the war was over in the publication of a magnificent series of volumes describing Egypt and its past, a new dimension was added to the world of learning. The fact that the British defeated the French in the field meant that many of their archaeological discoveries, such as the Rosetta Stone, found a home in the British Museum, not the Louvre. At the same time the Egyptian adventure changed the style of fashionable furniture throughout Europe.

At bottom, however, the motive for the expedition was one of personal ambition. Bonaparte was twenty-nine years old, his star had risen and he recalled that Alexander the Great had conquered the East before

that age. 'Europe is a molehill', he told his secretary, Bourrienne. 'Everything wears out; my glory is already past; this tiny Europe does not offer enough of it. We must go to the East; all great glory has always been gained there.'

The idea appealed to the Directory because it offered a chance of replacing its losses in the West Indies and the Cape of Good Hope, which had belonged to its Dutch allies, with a new colony in Egypt. Moreover, there was a possibility of striking at the British in India, if contact could be made with Tippoo Sahib, Sultan of Mysore, who was at war with France's most persistent enemy. What made the government agree forthwith was that the plan afforded a pretext of getting Bonaparte out of France: the prospect of a victorious, popular young general unemployed at home was one which made members of the Directory nervous.

It is difficult to know which to admire most: the secrecy with which the expedition was planned, the efficiency with which it was prepared in ten weeks, or the completeness of the conquest, at least on land. Few of those who sailed knew what their destination was, nor did the British guess the direction of this new move in the long war with the French Republic until after Bonaparte had won his first victory—the capture of Malta.

Ever since the Knights of St John of Jerusalem had been expelled from Rhodes by Suleyman the Magnificent in 1530 they had ruled the island of Malta and withstood many famous sieges on the part of the Turks. They were an international body dedicated to the destruction of the Ottoman Empire, and Europe had good reason to be grateful to them for fending off the threat of Islam for so long. But by 1798 they were a decadent order, unpopular with the islanders and divided amongst themselves. The fact that the Grand Master was an Austrian gave Bonaparte a pretext for destroying them. Of the 332 knights then alive, fifty were too old to fight and 200 were Frenchmen. For months past a fifth column had been infiltrated into Valletta, so that when the French arrived off the island on 9 June the impregnable fortress capitulated without a blow.

Compensation was offered to the knights, but they were expelled and their treasure, worth over a million livres, was confiscated. Between 12 June, the date of the surrender, and 19 June when Bonaparte sailed on to Egypt, Malta was entirely reorganised by 168 orders and proclamations. General Vaubois was left behind with a garrison of 3,000 men. How he withstood the siege of the British and the Maltese for the next two years is described in a later chapter of this book.

The significance of the events described in the following documents is thus not merely military or naval or cultural, but also political, on a grand scale.

The completeness of Nelson's victory altered the whole complexion of the war and resulted in the formation of a new coalition against the French Republic. In a wider view, the French invasion was the first occasion when the Arab world confronted the West on the field of battle and in the arena of European civilisation generally. It was not only the shock of military defeat which overturned the ancient order of things in the heart of the Middle East, but the innovation of such technological devices as the printing press, first brought to Cairo by the French. It is for such reasons that historians date the Arab Awakening from these events. If the ancient civilisation of Egypt was first uncovered by those who participated in the Nile Campaign, they were also responsible for bringing to birth a new power in the context of world history.

CHAPTER ONE

THE CAPTURE OF MALTA (1798)

The Plan Conceived

Bonaparte first suggested an expedition to Malta and Egypt in a LETTER TO TALLEYRAND, *Minister of Foreign Affairs in the Directory, when he was engaged in negotiating the Treaty of Campo Formio to conclude his victorious First Italian Campaign. He wrote from his headquarters, Passariano on the Venetian mainland, on 13 September 1797:*

Why should we not occupy the island of Malta? Admiral Brueys could easily anchor there and take it. Four hundred knights and, at the most, a regiment of 500 men are the sole defence of the town of Valletta. The inhabitants, of whom there are more than 100,000, are very well disposed to us and thoroughly disgusted with their knights, who are dying of hunger. I have purposely had all their possessions in Italy confiscated. With the island of St. Pierre, which the King of Sardinia has ceded to us, Malta, Corfu, etc., we shall be masters of the Mediterranean.

If it happens that when we make peace with England we have to give up the Cape of Good Hope, we must occupy Egypt. That country has never belonged to a European nation. The Venetians alone had a certain, but very precarious preponderance there several centuries ago. We would leave here with 25,000 men, escorted by 8 or 10 ships of the line or Venetian frigates, and take it. Egypt does not really belong to the Sultan.

I shall be glad to know, Citizen Minister, if you will enquire in Paris and let me know what reaction our expedition to Egypt would produce at the Porte. With armies such as ours, for which all religions are alike, Mohammedan, Copts, Arabs, pagans etc., all that is unimportant; we would respect one as much as the other.

I salute you.　　　　　　　　　　　　　　　**(1)**

The Directory promptly approved of Bonaparte's scheme, partly because the acquisition of a new colony would replace its losses in the West Indies and the Cape of Good Hope, but chiefly because it would rid

France for a time of an ambitious and successful young general. TALLEYRAND'S REPLY TO BONAPARTE *from Paris on 23 September 1797:*

The Directory approves of your ideas with regard to Malta. Since that Order has elected Monsieur de Hompesch as Grand Master the suspicions of the Directory are confirmed, based on the previous information, that Austria is desirous of gaining possession of that island. She is anxious to become a maritime power in the Mediterranean; it was for that purpose that at the preliminaries at Leoben she demanded before all else that portion of the Italian coast. Again, her haste to possess herself of Dalmatia, which is further proved by her avidity in taking Ragusa. Besides all this, the Neapolitan government is entirely under her influence. Malta for her would have a double advantage; it would serve to attract to her all the products of Sicily. It is not only on commercial grounds that she is desirous of retiring from the centre of Italy towards its coastline, but in view of contemplated conquests she is in truth arranging the means of attack on Turkish territory where Albania and Bosnia join her own, so that in concert with Russia she could attack these said provinces in the rear in the event of the Russian fleet entering the Archipelago. It is to our interests that such maritime extension on the part of Austria be stopped, and the Directory accordingly desires that you will take the necessary steps to prevent Malta falling into her hands.

With regard to Egypt, your views in this respect are grand, and their usefulness must be recognised . . . Egypt as a colony would soon compensate for the loss of the Antilles and open a road to us for obtaining the trade of India.   (2)

The Expeditionary Force

The force asked by Bonaparte was, in the event, actually exceeded, so that when the expedition sailed it consisted of 30,000 infantry, 3,000 cavalry, 300 transport vessels, 13 ships of the line and 7 frigates under Admiral Brueys, together with a further 20,000 troops joining from the Italian ports. He sent his PROPOSALS TO THE DIRECTORY *on 5 March 1798:*

To occupy Egypt and Malta would require from 20,000 to 25,000 infantry and from 2,000 to 3,000 dismounted cavalry. These troops could be found and embarked in France and Italy. The cavalry with harness, but without horses, each man armed with a musket.

All units with their (forward) depots.

One hundred cartridges per man.

Water on board for a month; food for two months.

These troops would have to be embarked in the various ports and ready to move at the beginning of Floréal (May) proceeding to the gulf of Ajaccio and assembled ready to leave there before the end of Floréal.

To these troops must be added: 60 field guns, 40 heavy siege guns; two companies of sappers; an artillery battalion; two companies of labourers; a pontoon battalion, which would be embarked in French and Italian ports as follows . . .

At Toulon we have six ships of the line and some frigates and corvettes; six tartanes mounting cannon must be added. Together, these ships would be sufficient to carry the troops to be embarked at Toulon.

According to the report of the Minister of Marine, this squadron will be ready to sail in a fortnight, though it lacks seamen. Therefore, it is necessary only to embargo and charter the ships necessary to transport the artillery.

To succeed in this expedition an extraordinary expenditure of five millions must be envisaged, apart from the ordinary expenses for supplying, arming and paying the fleet, for the pay, food and clothing of the troops, and for the cost of the artillery and engineers, which it is essential to equip effectively; that means in all a sum of from eight to nine millions to be borne by the Government between now and the 20th Germinal. (3)

The British Receive Intelligence

This LETTER, *which came into the hands of the British government in May, was the first rumour that Egypt was Bonaparte's destination. Its author was a distinguished mineralogist, Gratet de Dolomieu, who gave his name to the Dolomites, and it was dated 11 April 1798:*

The object of this grand voyage is not known; among the *savants*, only Bertholet knows it. What is certain is that they are going to embark at Toulon and Genoa, and that they are probably part of the military expedition which is in preparation. It is also certain that they have an immense amount of printing equipment, books, instruments, chemical apparatus which suggests a very long absence. Among the books one notices above everything travels to the Levant, Egypt, Persia, India, Turkey, the Black Sea, the Caspian, the travels of Anacharsis in Greece. They are taking a dozen geographical engineers, military engineers, mathematicians, astronomers, chemists, doctors, artists and naturalists of every sort; two professors of Arabic, Persian and Turkish, and all have gone on board without knowing where they are going.

Guesses baffle everyone. Some say a conquest in Egypt and cutting the Isthmus of Suez is contemplated in order to undermine English commerce with India; others think the operation will be a long one because another fleet of boats in pieces has been shipped for transportation to Suez in order to have a fleet in the Red Sea in fifteen days; others again suppose that English possessions in India are to be attacked by land, having crossed the desert, Persia and 'Mogol' with 30,000 men. It is said that Bonaparte will probably command the expedition. What is certain is that he is the chief promoter of the enterprise, and that he takes a lively interest in it. (4)

The Directory's Secret Decree

The Directory appointed Bonaparte commander-in-chief and empowered him to seize Malta and invade Egypt by a SECRET DECREE *dated 12 April 1798:*

The Executive Directory, considering that the Beys who have seized the government of Egypt have formed the most intimate ties with the English and have made themselves wholly dependent on them; that in consequence they have committed open hostilities and the most horrible cruelties towards Frenchmen, whom they daily molest, rob and murder.

Considering that it is its duty to pursue the enemies of the Republic wherever they may be found.

Considering furthermore that the infamous treachery by which England has made itself master of the Cape of Good Hope, having rendered access to India by the normal route very difficult for the ships of the Republic, it is necessary to open another route thither for the Republican forces, to combat the satellites for the English government there and to stop that source of its corrupting wealth;

DECREES

Article 1. The Commander-in-Chief of the Army of the East will lead the land and sea forces under his command to Egypt and will take possession of that country.

Article 2. He will drive the English from all their oriental possessions which he can reach, and notably he will destroy their settlements in the Red Sea.

Article 3. He will cause the isthmus of Suez to be cut through and he will take all necessary measures to ensure to the French Republic the free and exclusive possession of the Red Sea. (5)

Orders to Prepare the Fleet

Bonaparte sent INSTRUCTIONS TO VICE-ADMIRAL BRUEYS *from Paris on 22 April 1798:*

1 *Vice Admiral Brueys, Commander-in-Chief of the French fleet*

It is essential, Citizen Admiral, that you organize the fleet at once.

Commodore Ganteaume will carry out the functions of chief of staff of the fleet. Citizen Casabianca will be your flag captain . . .

Our thirteen ships of the line will be divided into three squadrons. Those of the right and left will each contain four ships, the centre, five. Each squadron will have a frigate and a corvette.

Rear-Admirals Blanquet du Chayla and Villeneuve will each command a squadron.

Rear-Admiral Decrès will command the convoy and will have under his orders two first rates . . . three frigates and a number of fast brigs which you will select. With these ships he will lead the movement and will be ready to command the light squadron which you may decide to form by detaching ships from the fleet.

But, once the enemy is in sight and the line of battle formed, all Admiral Decrès's care, with his frigates, will be for convoy, to attend to its safety and carry out the orders you may have given him. **(6)**

BONAPARTE'S EMBARKATION SPEECH *to his troops at Toulon is a good example of his military oratory, though his promises became a joke in the army after it had landed in Egypt. The official newspaper* Moniteur *denied that he had made this speech. but other sources confirm it.*

Officers and soldiers, two years ago I came to take command of you. At that time, you were on the Ligurian coast, in the greatest want, lacking everything, having sold even your watches to provide for your needs. There all was given to you in abundance. Have I not kept my word? (Shouts of 'Yes'.) Well, let me tell you that I have not done enough yet for the fatherland, nor the fatherland for you. I

2 *A stern view of a model of a French 120-gun ship.* L'Orient, *the flagship in which Napoleon sailed, must have looked much like this. Sne carried over 1,000 men, and was larger than any ship in the Royal Navy*

shall now lead you into a country where by your future deeds you will surpass even those that are now astonishing your admirers, and you will render to the Republic such services as she has a right to expect from an invincible army. I promise every soldier that upon his return to France, he shall have enough to buy himself six acres of land. (Shouts of 'Long live the immortal Republic!') **(7)**

Malta is Alerted
The first warning that an attack on Malta was intended was sent by the ambassador of the Knights of St John who was attending a conference in Austria. It was received on 4 June, a week before the attack took place, but owing to the machinations of the French knights no steps were taken to defend the island. The LETTER *was dated 18 May 1798:*

MONSEIGNEUR, I have to acquaint you that the formidable expedition now preparing at Toulon is intended for the capture of Malta and Egypt. I have this information from the Secretary of M. Treilhard, one of the French Republican Ministers at the congress. You will most assuredly be attacked. Take all necessary steps for your defence. All the Ministers of the various powers attending this congress, friends of the Order, have the same intelligence, but they also know that the fortress of Malta is impregnable, or at least capable of resisting a three months siege. The honour of Your Eminence, and the preservation of the Order, are at stake, and if you surrender without making any defence, you will be dishonoured in the eyes of Europe. Moreover, this expedition is regarded here as a disgrace inflicted on Bonaparte, who has two powerful enemies in the Directory who fear him, and have so arranged that he should now be removed to a distance. These members of the Directory are Rewbell and La Révellière-Lepaux. **(8)**

The Expedition Underway
On the way to Malta the fleet passed near Bastia in

Corsica, the town near Ajaccio where Napoleon and Joseph Bonaparte were born. As a member of the Council of Five Hundred, Joseph was his brother's chief confidant in Paris and the following LETTER FROM NAPOLEON was written on board L'Orient on 23 May 1798:

We have joined the convoy from Genoa; we have had good, bad, and calm weather. We are well on our way, moving towards Elba. This evening we shall be opposite Bastia. I have not been sea-sick.

Please send me news. I wrote to you from Toulon what I wish you to do. What concerns you in the arrangement I made with you goes well. I salute you.

P.S. My wife will wait a few days at Toulon, until she knows that we have passed Sicily; after that she will go to take the waters.

General Vaubois, to whom these ORDERS *were sent, commanded the attacking force and was later left as commander-in-chief of the garrison at Malta. The orders were sent by Napoleon from* L'Orient *before Malta on 11 June 1798:* **(9)**

The Commander-in-Chief understands, General, that the Grand Master of the Order of Jerusalem has informed the French military commander that there is an armistice. There are only parleys, in the town and on board *L'Orient*. If the armistice takes place, it will be for the fortress, unless the other positions of the island are specifically mentioned.

The Commander-in-Chief hopes that during the course of the day you will become master of the Old City and of the whole island, in accordance with the orders you received yesterday from the Commander-in-Chief. **(10)**

Defence and Capture

The next four documents show how feeble the defence

3 *A contemporary model of a French frigate of the type in action during the Battle of the Nile*

of Malta was. *The first is from the memoirs of* DOUBLET, *the secretary of Hompesch, the Grand Master. The second was written by* GRATET DE DOLOMIEU, *one of the savants. The third comes from the memoirs of Napoleon's secretary,* FAUVELET DE BOURRIENNE. *The last is from the memoirs of* GENERAL MARMONT, *who had a treacherous French knight as his guide in an attack on a key position.*

From the Palace to my residence there may be the distance of two to three hundred yards, and arriving at the corner of the Carmelite church I there found acting as sentinel the lawyer Torregiani, a neighbour of mine, who I asked, 'What are you doing there? Are you guarding the Madonna' (whose statue was just above him)?' He replied, 'I know what I am doing, but I fear very much that the Grand Master knows not what he is doing. They are firing away; but to what purpose? It can only alarm women and children. It would be far better if the Council would consider and verify whether they have sufficient forces to resist the assault which the French are capable of attempting this very night; as for me, I am of opinion that all the Bailiffs and Knights, as well as the Grand Master, lost their heads when they refused water to Bonaparte. The entire country is now in the possession of the enemy; what can be worse? Do they wish the city to be taken and sacked, our churches profaned, our wives and children violated, and ourselves killed?'

Continuing my way homewards, Torregiani remarked: 'Instead of sighing as you do, it would be better for you to tell me frankly what is your opinion, for I have told you mine, as to what we Maltese should do under these circumstances'. 'To reply with confidence on the operations of the Order, as good and faithful subjects', I replied.

'What? Sacrifice ourselves for a handful of degenerate and panic-stricken Knights, who know not how to defend, govern, or command us!' 'It is useless', I replied, 'for you to address these words to me, for I am of no account'. 'To whom, then, should they be addressed?' 'My duty, like yours', I observed, 'is to respect authority, and to keep silent'.

'Well and good; if you intend to keep silent, I shall not, and from this moment I shall go and seek the Jurists, and ascertain what they are doing'. We thereupon separated, and I retired to my house . .

After a rough passage we reached *L'Orient* about midnight, to find that Bonaparte and his staff had retired for the night, but within half an hour the interview was granted. Bonaparte personally drafted the articles, which out of consideration for the honour of the Knights, he desired should be called a Convention. Ex-Auditor Muscat asked for an additional article, to the effect that the exceptions and privileges of his Nation should be guaranteed.

Bonaparte, much amused, declared that 'privileges no longer existed, nor corporations, and that the law was the same for all'. The Bailli Frisari had some scruples in signing the convention, and requested his colleague Ransijat to be his interpreter with the General. He desired to reserve by a memorandum under his signature the rights of his sovereign the King of Naples on the Isle of Malta, believing that if he did not do so he would be punished, by the confiscation of his commanderies. 'You may', replied Bonaparte, 'make use of all the reserve you please, we shall be ready to render them null and void by cannon-shot'. **(11)**

When the attack was made the Grand Master wrote to me to ask the General what he wanted and what were the conditions he demanded from the Order, and requested me to use my good offices with him. The General opened the letter and told me to come on board.

'Here is a letter which shows that you have some influence in Malta', he said. 'I am come here to seize Malta, but I have no time to lose. I have information that there is an English squadron at Sardinia and I

wish to anticipate its appearance. Malta has no means of defending itself. The Maltese don't wish to obey the Knights, whom they despise and have already assassinated many of them. Therefore resistance cannot last long. But, as I say, I don't want to lose time. Tell the Knights I will grant them most advantageous conditions; that I want to purchase the island; that I will pay what they want, whether in cash or by the treaty I will make with them, that all the French can return to France and enjoy their political rights; that those who wish to remain in Malta will be protected; that the Grand Master can have a principality in Germany and anything he wishes. If it is really necessary, you can offer to preserve the Order at Malta, provided the port is handed over to us, and we can garrison the city; that won't worry us much. You will tell the government of Malta that we are forced to take these measures because of the engagements the island has made with Russia, which we cannot tolerate'.

I left for Malta with Junot, the aide-de-camp, and Poussielgue. We arrived at one o'clock in the afternoon. I persuaded the Grand Master that he must sacrifice the island and depend on the generosity of Bonaparte for conditions; that the quicker he handed Malta over to us, the better the General would be pleased. The Council assembled to nominate plenipotentiaries for the negotiations and at six o'clock we left for Malta to return to *L'Orient*, which we reached at eleven in the evening because of bad weather.

As soon as the attack was made and the Grand Master wished to try out his means of defence, the suspicions sown earlier produced their effect. The Maltese said they would never obey the French Knights, who wished to hand them over to their

4 *Nelson's shortage of frigates, fast reconnaissance vessels such as the one illustrated by this model, made it possible for the French to reach Egypt undetected*

compatriots; they were traitors and thirteen were killed or wounded. Any attempt at defence was henceforward impossible for fear that the Maltese would massacre all the French Knights, and this fear hastened the negotiations . . .

The treaty was made and signed in half an hour because, it was said, it would be necessary to have additional articles inserted in a document drawn up with so much haste. These articles have never been drawn up and none of the conditions were executed. The Knights were ordered to leave Malta in three days. No passports were issued to anyone who had not been resident for seven years, and all the help promised them was reduced to 250 livres per person, which totalled 50,000 apart from the sum paid for the household of the Grand Master.

After having demanded that Malta should be sold to him, Bonaparte could not have got it cheaper. **(12)**

The intrigues had not succeeded in causing the ports of the island to be opened to us immediately on arrival. Bonaparte expressed much displeasure against the persons sent from Europe to arrange measures for that purpose. One of them, M. Dolomieu, had cause to repent his mission. M. Poussielgue had done all he could but had not completely succeeded. There was some misunderstanding and in consequence some shots were fired . . . But as every person in the secret knew, this was a mere form and these hostile demonstrations produced no unpleasant consequences. We wished to save the honour of the Knights, that was all; for no one who has seen Malta can imagine that an island surrounded with such formidable fortifications would have surrendered in two days to a fleet pursued by an enemy. The impregnable fortress of Malta is so secure against a *coup de main* that General Caffarelli, after examining its fortifications, said to the General in my presence, 'Upon my word, General, it is lucky that there is some one in the town to open the gates for us'. **(13)**

If the Maltese Government had performed its duty, if the French Knights had not made sorties such as that described with a Militia undrilled, to meet a numerous and veteran enemy, and had been content to remain behind their ramparts, the strongest in Europe, we should not have gained entrance. The English fleet in our wake would have quickly destroyed ours, or put it to flight, and with the army landed wanting in every necessity, would in a few days have been suffering the pangs of famine, and compelled to surrender. There is no exaggeration in this picture, it is the simple truth, and one trembles to think of such risks which might so easily have been anticipated, so capriciously encountered by a brave army; but the hand of Providence was guarding us, and preserved us from such a catastrophe. **(14)**

The Surrender
Bosredon-Ransijat, the French knight who signed this CONVENTION *on the surrender of Malta, was rewarded by being appointed to the governing committee. On board* L'Orient *before Malta 21 June 1798:*
Convention agreed between the French Republic, represented by Citizen Bonaparte, Commander-in-Chief, of the one part, and the Order of the Knights of St John of Jerusalem.
Article 1. The Knights of the Order of St John of Jerusalem will deliver the forts of Malta to the French army. They renounce in favour of the French Republic their rights of sovereignty over this town and the islands of Malta, Gozo and Comino.
Article 2. The French Republic will use its influence at the Congress of Rastadt to secure to the Grand Master, during his lifetime, a principality equivalent to that which he loses hereby, and meanwhile it undertakes to pay him an annual pension of 300,000 francs; in addition he will be given the value of two years' duration of this pension as indemnity for

5 *A below-decks section of a ship of the line*

his personal property. So long as he remains at Malta he will retain the military honours which he formerly enjoyed.

Article 3. The Knights of the Order who are French, at present at Malta, and of whom a list will be drawn up by the Commander-in-Chief, may return to their country and their residence in Malta will be counted to them as residence in France. The French Republic will use its good offices with the Cisalpine, Roman, Ligurian and Helvetic Republics to have the present Article declared applicable to the Knights of these different nations. **(15)**

French Rule Established

The government of Malta was entirely reorganised by ORDERS AND PROCLAMATIONS *issued during the next week, of which the following, dated 13 June 1798, are examples:*

Bonaparte, Commander-in-Chief, member of the Institute, orders:

1. The islands of Malta and Gozo will be administered by a governing committee composed of nine persons, to be appointed by the Commander-in-Chief.

2. A French commissioner will be attached to the governing committee.

3. The governing committee will at once commence organising civil and criminal courts, following as far as possible the forms at present existing in France. Appointment of members of the courts will require approval of the general officer commanding in Malta. Until these courts are organised, justice will continue to be administered as in the past.

4. All the properties of the Order of Malta, of the Grand Master and the different monasteries of the Knights belong to the French Republic.

5. The police will be wholly under the orders of the

6, 7 & 8 *A purser, midshipman and captain of the Royal Navy by Rowlandson*

general officer commanding and the officers under his orders.

6.   The following citizens to compose the governing committee—Bosredon-Ransijat . . .

7.   The officers and soldiers who composed the military forces in the service of the Order of Malta will assemble at 2.0 p.m. today and will proceed to Bircarcara at 5.0 a.m. tomorrow.

8.   All armorial bearings will be removed within twenty-four hours. It is forbidden to wear livery or any mark or title of nobility.

9.   All Knights and inhabitants who are subject of a power at war with France, such as Russia and Portugal, are required to leave Malta within forty-eight hours.   **(16)**

The Plunder of Malta

French Republican armies invariably plundered the states which they conquered. In the case of Malta, the mineralogist Berthollet, Member of the Institute, was in charge and the treasure was stowed on board the flagship L'Orient, *so that it went to the bottom at the Battle of the Nile. It included twelve statues of the Apostles in silver, but the silver gates of the church of St John escaped because they happened to be painted over at the time. Bonaparte, Commander-in-Chief, gave*

the ORDERS FOR CONFISCATION *on 13 June 1798:*

Article 1.   Citizen Berthollet, the auditor of the Army and a clerk to the Paymaster, will take possession of the gold, silver and precious stones which are in the church of St John and other dependencies of the Order of Malta, the silverware of the hotels and that of the Grand Master.

2.   During the course of tomorrow they will have all the gold cast into ingots to be transferred to the chest of the Army Paymaster.

3.   They will make an inventory of all the precious stones which will be placed under seal in the Army chest.

4.   They will sell silverware worth 250,000 to 300,000 francs to local merchants for gold and silver money, which will also be placed in the Army chest.

5.   The rest of the silverware will be left at the Maltese mint to be coined, and the money will be transmitted to the divisional Paymaster for the upkeep of this division; it will be specified how much this will produce, so that the Paymaster can be accountable for it.

6.   They will leave what is necessary for the exercise of the cult at the church of St John and the other churches.   **(17)**

CHAPTER TWO

THE BATTLE OF THE NILE (1798)

Bonaparte's victories in Italy and the alliance of Spain with France compelled the British fleet under Sir John Jervis (created Earl St Vincent after his defeat of the Spanish fleet on 14 February 1797) to evacuate the Mediterranean. Over a year later, on 2 May 1798, a re-entry into that sea was made when Nelson was sent to watch Toulon by his commander-in-chief. By so doing, St Vincent anticipated instructions from his government. Spencer, First Lord of the Admiralty, and Dundas, Secretary of War, were convinced that something was afoot at Toulon, though they had no idea what Bonaparte was planning. It was feared that the French fleet might be coming round to Brest for another attempt at an invasion of Ireland, as in the previous year. Moreover, Pitt was trying to form a Second Coalition against France. It was for these reasons that Spencer told St Vincent that 'the appearance of a British squadron in the Mediterranean is a condition on which the fate of Europe at this moment may be stated to depend'.

But Nelson had with him only three 74-gun ships and two frigates, and soon after his arrival before Toulon a gale drove him south to Sardinia. The opportunity was seized for the French expedition to sail, while Nelson's frigates deserted him for Gibraltar, imagining that he must go there for repairs to his flagship after the storm. When he returned to Toulon he found the French gone and for the rest of the campaign the lack of frigates deprived him of the 'eyes' of the fleet. On 7 June, however, Troubridge arrived with reinforcements, so that with a fleet of fifteen sail of the line he could go in pursuit of the French. By that date Bonaparte was approaching Malta.

It was not until he heard of the fall of that island from Sir William Hamilton, British Ambassador at the court of Naples and Sicily, that Nelson had any inkling what the destination of the French might be. He was the first to guess that it might be Egypt.

Then followed a second misfortune. The two

25

fleets passed each other on a south-easterly course during the night of 22-23 June off Crete, Nelson's faster rate of sailing enabling him to reach Alexandria on 29 June. It was a lucky escape for the French, because their huge armament would have been no match for the British fleet, the best that was ever seen in the Mediterranean, even though it lacked frigates. Since there was no sign of the French, Nelson made off for the Levant. Twenty-four hours later Bonaparte arrived at Alexandria.

'All my ill-fortune has proceeded from want of frigates', Nelson told Hamilton, as he searched desperately in the eastern Mediterranean. He was back at Syracuse on 20 July, where he received the first definite information that the destination of the French was indeed Egypt.

On 1 August he arrived at Alexandria a second time. There he learned that the French fleet lay at anchor in Aboukir Bay, a few miles to the east. During the long chase he had taken the opportunity to discuss with his captains, his Band of Brothers, as he called them, to pool their ideas in order to give maximum opportunity for the exercise of their initiative, should they ever catch up with the enemy. So, although the leading ships rounded Aboukir point at two o'clock in the afternoon, an immediate attack on the French was made at six with only two hours daylight left.

This was the last thing that Brueys expected. Not only were many of his seamen on shore collecting water, but the port-side guns of his ships were not even manned. His thirteen ships of the line stretched in a bow across the bay, with the frigates lying inshore. The ships lay about 200 yards apart to allow them to swing at their anchor buoys. To Nelson and his leading captain, Foley of the *Goliath*, it appeared that where there was room for a French ship to swing there was room for a British ship to anchor. So the five leading ships passed inside the French line, Nelson's *Vanguard* being the first to attack from the seaward side.

The battle, which was fought in gathering darkness, was the most spontaneous in the history of warfare under sail. Every captain felt for an opponent, except Troubridge in the *Culloden*, who had run aground after taking the corner of Aboukir point too sharply. They had no charts, so that only their initiative and determination won the victory. The French flagship *L'Orient* was much larger than any British ship, but having beaten off the *Bellerophon* she was attacked on either quarter by the *Swiftsure* and *Alexander*, so that at ten o'clock she blew up. Brueys had fought his ship most gallantly before he was literally cut in two by a shot and his captain Casabianca was also killed. It was the death of the latter's son which inspired the Victorian ballad 'The boy stood on the burning deck, whence all but he had fled'.

The loss of the flagship was the deciding event of the night, though the action continued until dawn. By then only the three rear enemy ships under the command of Villeneuve (whom Nelson was to meet again at Trafalgar) escaped. One of them ran aground; another was later captured; but the *Genereux* captured HMS *Leander* in the Adriatic before she was herself taken.

The Battle of the Nile was the most complete victory in naval history, and this demonstration of sea power had important political consequences. The Second Coalition was formed shortly afterwards with the Austrian army reconquering northern Italy. The Ottoman and Russian empires entered the war on the British side. Malta was cut off. As for Egypt, Nelson said, 'Their army is in a scrape, and will not get out of it'. To Bonaparte the defeat was indeed a challenge. As he told his staff, 'Now, gentlemen, we are obliged to accomplish great things. The sea, of which we are no longer masters, separates us from our homeland, but no sea separates us from either Africa or Asia'. This was the reason for his attempt to escape from Egypt by way of Syria; but there again (as will be seen in Chapter Four) sea power blocked his way at Acre.

The British enter the Mediterranean

The following orders from Edward Nepean, Secretary of the Admiralty, and the covering LETTER FROM LORD SPENCER, *First Lord of the Admiralty, reached Admiral the Earl of St Vincent, commander-in-chief of the fleet blockading the Spanish at Cadiz, on 10 May. On 2 May, however, St Vincent had anticipated the instructions by sending Nelson in command of a small squadron of observation, into the Mediterranean. He was there reinforced by the ships mentioned by Spencer. It will be noticed that Egypt as the destination of the Toulon armament remained a profound secret for the British government. One of the consequences of Nelson's victory at the Battle of the Nile was the formation of a Second Coalition with Austria, as indicated in Spencer's letter from the Admiralty on 29 April 1798:*

My dear Lord—You will by the present conveyance receive a letter from Nepean preparing you for orders to act upon a plan of operations very different from what we have hitherto adopted, and which I have no doubt will appear to be attended with a considerable degree of risk. You will easily conceive that such an instruction would not have been in contemplation if the circumstances in which we now find ourselves did not in a manner oblige us to take a measure of a more decided and hazardous complexion than we should otherwise have thought ourselves justified in taking; but when you are apprised that the appearance of a British squadron in the Mediterranean is a condition on which the fate of Europe may at this moment be stated to depend, you will not be surprised that we are disposed to strain every nerve and incur considerable hazard in effecting it. The armament of Toulon, Genoa, etc., is represented as being very extensive, and is very probably in the first instance intended for Naples. The apprehension of this, added to other reasons of various kinds, have pro-

duced a disposition on the part of Austria towards the French Republic which is almost sure to end in an open rupture, and the Austrians are in great force on the confines of Italy. This armament is in truth more likely to be destined for Portugal or Ireland; for the former most probably, by landing somewhere in Spain; for the latter, by pushing through the Straits and escaping our vigilance, which, while you are occupied by the fleet at Cadiz, it is not impossible they may succeed in. Whatever its destination its defeat would surely be a great object for this country, and it is with that view in the first instance that the instructions are sent, of which you now have notice . . .

It is proposed to be left to your Lordship's determination whether this purpose should be obtained by a detachment from your fleet or by taking your whole force into the Mediterranean. At the same time I cannot help suggesting it would be extremely desirable not to lose sight of the great advantage which has hitherto been obtained from the constant check which you have kept on the Spanish fleet at Cadiz. We are inclined to hope that you may find it practicable to send a detachment into the Mediterranean sufficiently strong to attain that end, and at the same time remain in a situation to watch with effect the fleet at Cadiz, till by reinforcement we can again put you in a state to block that port in the manner you have done before. If you determine to send a detachment into the Mediterranean, I think it almost unnecessary to suggest to you the propriety of putting it under the command of Sir H. Nelson, whose acquaintance with that port of the world as well as his activity and disposition seem to qualify him in a peculiar manner for that service. We shall take care to send you out ships which are the best suited for foreign service of any which we have to dispose of, in order to make your fleet as effective as possible, and I trust that the first division of the reinforcements intended for you will reach you so soon as not to have given time to the enemy to

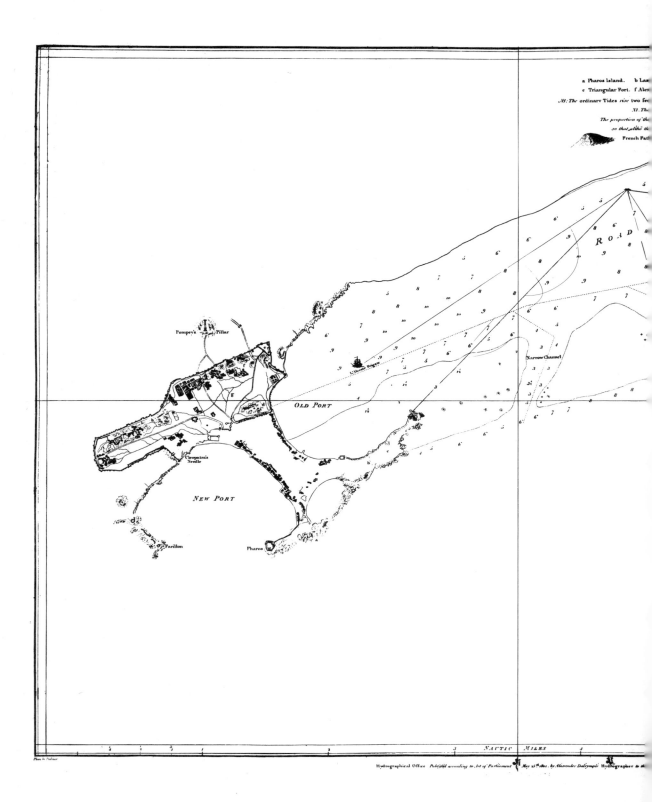

Hydrographical Office. Published according to Act of Parliament. May 25th 1801. by Alexander Dalrymple Hydrographer to the

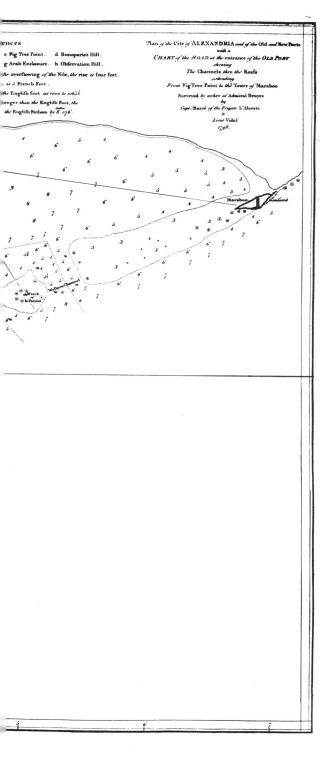

Plan of the City of ALEXANDRIA and of the Old and New Ports

with a

CHART of the ROAD at the entrance of the OLD PORT

shewing

The Channels thro the Reefs

extending

From Fig Tree Point to the Tower of Maraboo

Surveyed by order of Admiral Bruyes

by

Capt Barré of the Frigate L'Alceste

&

Lieut Vidal

1798.

combine any measures in consequence of this new disposition of our force . . .

I have thought it necessary to enter into this reasoning on this occasion to impress your Lordship with the great urgency and importance of the measure which has now been determined upon, and to justify our calling upon you to place yourself (at least for a short time) in a situation of more difficulty than any less pressing emergency would warrant us in doing, I am etc. SPENCER. **(18)**

ORDERS FROM THE SECRETARY OF THE ADMIRALTY *to St Vincent, dated 29 April 1798:*

My Lord, The present state of affairs rendering it absolutely necessary that the fleet and armament fitting out at Toulon should be prevented from accomplishing its object, which, from the information received, appears to be either an attack upon Naples and Sicily, or the conveyance of an army to some part of the coast of Spain, for the purpose of marching towards Portugal; or to pass through the Straits, with a view to proceeding to Ireland; my Lords Commissioners of the Admiralty have judged it expedient that I should apprise your Lordship that orders will be despatched to you in the course of a very few days, for sending into the Mediterranean a force which may be competent either to defeat, or at least delay, the departure of the said armament, in order that your Lordship may make the necessary arrangement for carrying their instructions to you into execution the moment of their arrival . . . NEPEAN. **(19)**

ST VINCENT'S INSTRUCTIONS TO NELSON *sent from Cadiz on 2 May 1798:*

Whereas I have received certain intelligence that a considerable armament is making at Toulon, and a number of transports collecting at Marseilles and

9 *One of the earliest British Admiralty charts of Alexandria. Published in 1801, this was based on a captured French survey of 1798*

Genoa for an embarkation of troops, You are hereby authorised and required to proceed with such of the squadron under your orders as may be at Gibraltar up the Mediterranean, and endeavour to ascertain by every means in your power, either upon the coasts of Provence or Genoa, the object of the equipment, the destination of which is differently spoken of—such as the islands of Sicily and Corfu on the one hand, Portugal or Ireland on the other, and in the latter event, that it is to join a squadron of Spanish ships said to be equipping at Cartagena; to which you will also have attention; and in case of your receiving any information which you may judge of importance to communicate to me, you are to despatch the *Bonne Citoyenne* or *Terpsichore* with it; and continue on this service, with the rest of the squadron, as long as you think necessary, and your stock of water will enable you to do, taking especial care, should this armament be coming down the Mediterranean, not to suffer it to pass the Straits before you, so as to prevent your joining me in time to impede a union between it and the Spanish fleet in Cadiz Bay. ST VINCENT.

(20)

The French Fleet Escapes From Toulon

Nelson was driven off Toulon on 19 May; the French left on 20 May; Nelson was back there again on 24 May, when he sent his REPORT TO ST VINCENT *from HMS* Vanguard *off the island of St Peter's in Sardinia:*
My Lord,

I am sorry to be obliged to inform you of the accidents which have happened to the *Vanguard*. On Saturday, May the 19th, it blew strong from the N.W. On Sunday it moderated so much, as to enable us to get our top-gallant masts and yards aloft. After dark it began to blow strong; but as the Ship was prepared for a gale, my mind was easy. At half past one A.M. on Monday, the main-top-mast went over the side, as did soon afterwards the mizen-mast. As it was impossible for any night-signal to be seen, I

A VIEW of the HARBOUR and CITY of ALEXANDRIA from the PHARO'S TOWER

had hopes we should be quiet till day-light, when I determined to wear, and scud before the gale; but about half-past three the fore-mast went in three pieces, and the bowsprit was found to be sprung in three places. When the day broke, we were fortunately enabled to wear the Ship with a remnant of the sprit-sail. The *Orion*, *Alexander*, and *Emerald* wore with head to the N.E., had we not wore, which was hardly to be expected, the Ship must have drifted to Corsica. The gale blew very hard all the day, and the Ship laboured most exceedingly. In the evening, being in latitude 40° 50' N., I determined to steer for Oristan Bay, in the Island of Sardinia: during the night, the *Emerald* parted company, for what reason I am at present unacquainted with. Being unable to get into Oristan, the *Alexander* took us in tow, and by Captain Ball's unremitting attention to our distress, and by Sir James Saumarez's exertions and ability in finding out the Island of St. Peter's and the proper anchorage, the *Vanguard* was, on May the 23rd, at noon, brought safely to an anchor into the harbour of St. Peter's. I have the honour to be, etc., HORATIO NELSON.   (21)

On the same day, 24 May 1798, Nelson sent a LETTER TO LADY NELSON:

My dearest Fanny, I ought not to call what has happened to the *Vanguard* by the cold name of accident: I believe firmly, that it was the Almighty's goodness, to check my consummate vanity. I hope it has made me a better Officer, as I feel confident it has made me a better Man. I kiss with all humility the rod.

Figure to yourself a vain man, on Sunday evening at sun-set, walking in his cabin with a Squadron about him, who looked up to their Chief to lead them to glory, and in whom this Chief placed the firmest reliance, that the proudest Ships, in equal numbers, belonging to France, would have bowed their Flags; and with a very rich Prize lying by him. Figure to yourself this proud, conceited man, when the sun rose on Monday morning, his Ship dismasted, his Fleet dispersed, and himself in such distress, that the meanest Frigate out of France would have been a very unwelcome guest. But it has pleased Almighty God to bring us into a safe Port, where, although we are refused the rights of humanity, yet the *Vanguard*

10 *A view of the harbour and city of Alexandria from the Pharaoh's Tower*

us; but the *Terpsichore, Bonne Citoyenne,* and a French Smyrna ship, continued to lay to under bare poles. Our situation was 25 leagues south of the Islands of Hières; and as we were laying with our will in two days get to sea again, as an English Man-of-War. (22)

The Chase to Egypt

The following five letters describe Nelson's vain chase of the French fleet, in which he was hampered by lack of frigates as scouting vessels. The first is to the British Ambassador in Sicily; the second to the British Consul at Alexandria; the third and fourth to his commander-in-chief explaining his dilemma and his intentions; and the last confessing that he has entirely failed to locate the enemy.

NELSON TO SIR WILLIAM HAMILTON *from HMS* Vanguard, *off Italy, 14 June 1798:*

My dear Sir, I have heard by a vessel just spoke with that the French fleet were seen off the north end of Sicily, steering to the eastward, on the 4th June. If they mean an attack on Sicily, I hope by this time they have barely made a landing, for if their fleet is not moored in as strong a port as Toulon, nothing shall hinder me from attacking them; and, with the blessing of Almighty God, I hope for a most glorious victory. I send Captain Troubridge to communicate with your Excellency, and, as Captain Troubridge is in full possession of my confidence, I beg that whatever he says may be considered as coming from me. Captain Troubridge is my honoured acquaintance for twenty-five years, and the very best sea-officer in His Majesty's service. I hope pilots will be with us in a few hours; for I will not lose one moment after the brig's return to wait for anything. Believe me, your Excellency's most obedient servant. HORATIO NELSON. (23)

NELSON TO GEORGE BALDWIN, CONSUL AT ALEXANDRIA *from HMS* Vanguard, *at sea, 26 June 1798:*

Sir, The French having possessed themselves of Malta, on Friday, the 15th of this month, the next day, the whole Fleet consisting of sixteen Sail of the Line, Frigates, Bomb vessels, etc., and near three hundred Transports, left the Island. I only heard this unpleasant news on the 22nd, off Cape Passaro. As Sicily was not their object, and the wind blew fresh from the westward, from the time they sailed, it was clear that their destination was to the eastward; and I think their object is to possess themselves of some Port in Egypt, and to fix themselves at the head of the Red Sea, in order to get a formidable Army into India; and, in concert with Tippoo Sahib, to drive us, if possible, from India. But I have reason to believe from not seeing a Vessel, that they have heard of my coming up the Mediterranean, and are got safe into Corfu. But still I am most exceedingly anxious to know from you if any reports or preparations have been made in Egypt for them; or any Vessels prepared in the Red Sea, to carry them to India, where, from the prevailing winds at this season, they would soon arrive; or any other information you would be good enough to give me, I shall hold myself much obliged. I am, Sir etc., HORATIO NELSON. (24)

NELSON TO ST VINCENT *from HMS* Vanguard, *at sea, 29 June 1798:*

Upon their whole proceedings, together with such information as I have been able to collect, it appeared clear to me, that either they were destined to assist the rebel Pacha and to overthrow the present Government of Turkey, or to settle a Colony in Egypt, and to open a trade to India by way of the Red Sea; for, strange as it may appear at first sight, an enterprising Enemy, if they have the force or consent of the Pacha of Egypt, may with great ease get an Army to the Red Sea, and if they have concerted a plan with Tippoo Sahib to have vessels at Suez, three weeks, at this season, is a common passage to the Malabar Coast, when our India possessions would be in great danger.

I therefore determined, with the opinion of those Captains in whom I place great confidence, to go to

Alexandria; and if that place, or any other part of Egypt was their destination, I hope to arrive in time enough to frustrate their plans. The only objection I can fancy to be stated is, 'you should not have gone such a long voyage without more certain information of the Enemy's destination': my answer is ready—who was I to get it from? The Governments of Naples and Sicily either knew not, or chose to keep me in ignorance. Was I to wait patiently till I heard certain accounts? If Egypt was their object before I could hear of them they would have been in India. To do nothing, I felt, was disgraceful: therefore I made use of my understanding, and by it I ought to stand or fall. I am before your Lordship's judgement (which in the present case I feel is the Tribunal of my Country), and if, under all circumstances, it is decided that I am wrong, I ought, for the sake of our Country, to be superseded; for, at this moment, when I know the French are not in Alexandria, I hold the same opinion as off Cape Passaro—viz, that under all circumstances, I was right in steering for Alexandria, and by that opinion I must stand or fall. However erroneous my judgment may be, I feel conscious of my honest intentions, which I hope will bear me up under the greatest misfortune that could happen to me as an Officer— that of your Lordship's thinking me wrong. I have the honour to be, with the highest respect, Your Lordship's most obedient Servant, HORATIO NELSON. (25)

NELSON TO ST VINCENT *from HMS* Vanguard *at Syracuse on 20 July 1798:*
My Lord, From my letter of the 12th you will be informed of my conduct to that time. I have now to acquaint you that having spoke several vessels from the westward, and one from Corfu, I know, as far as their reports, that the French are neither to the Westward of Sicily nor at Corfu. Yesterday I arrived here, where I can learn no more than vague conjecture that the French are gone to the eastward. Every moment I have to regret the Frigates having left me, to which must be attributed my ignorance of the movements of the Enemy. Your Lordship deprived yourself of Frigates to make mine certainly the first Squadron in the world, and I feel that I have zeal and activity to do credit to your appointment, and yet to be unsuccessful hurts me most sensibly. But if they are above water, I will find them out, and if possible bring them to battle. You have done your part in giving me so fine a Fleet, and I hope to do mine in making use of them. We are watering, and getting such refreshments as the place affords, and shall get to sea by the 25th. (Actually 23rd). It is my intention to get into the mouth of the Archipelago, where, if the Enemy are gone towards Constantinople, we shall hear of them directly: if I get no information there, to go to Cyprus, when, if they are in Syria or Egypt, I must hear of them. Seventeen Sail of the Line, eight Frigates, etc., of War, went from Malta with them. We have a report that on the 1st of July, the French were seen off Candia, but near what part of the Island I cannot learn. I have the honour to remain etc., HORATIO NELSON. (26)

NELSON TO SIR WILLIAM HAMILTON *from HMS* Vanguard *at Syracuse on 20 July 1798:*
My dear Sir, It is an old saying, 'the Devil's children have the Devil's luck'. I cannot find, or to this moment learn, beyond vague conjecture where the French Fleet are gone to. All my ill fortune, hitherto, has proceeded from want of Frigates. Off Cape Passaro, on the 22nd of June, at day-light, I saw two Frigates, which were supposed to be French, and it has been said since that a Line of Battle Ship was to leeward of them, with the riches of Malta on board, but it was the destruction of the Enemy, not riches for myself, that I was seeking. These would have fallen to me if I had had Frigates, but except the Ship of the Line, I regard not all the riches in this world.

From every information off Malta I believed they were gone to Egypt. Therefore, on the 28th, I was communicating with Alexandria in Egypt, where I found the Turks preparing to resist them, but know nothing beyond report. From thence I stretched over to the coast of Caramania (Levant) where, not meeting a Vessel that could give me information, I became distressed for the Kingdom of the Two Sicilies, and having gone a round of 600 leagues at this season of the year (with a single Ship) with an expedition incredible, here I am as ignorant of the situation of the Enemy as I was twenty-seven days ago. I sincerely hope that the Dispatches which I understand are at Cape Passaro will give me full information. I shall be able for nine or ten weeks longer to keep the Fleet on active service, when we shall want provisions and stores. I send a paper on that subject herewith. Mr. Littledale, is, I suppose, sent up by the Admiral to victual us, and I hope he will do it cheaper than any other person; but if I find out that he charges more than the fair price, and has not the provisions of the very best quality, I will not take them; for, as no Fleet has more fag than this, nothing but the best food and greatest attention can keep them healthy. At this moment, we have not one sick man in the Fleet. In about six days I shall sail from hence, and if I hear nothing more from the French, I shall go to the Archipelago, where if they are gone towards Constantinople I shall hear of them. I shall go to Cyprus, and if they are gone to Alexandretta, or any other part of Syria or Egypt, I shall get information. You will, I am sure, and so will our country, easily conceive what has passed in my anxious mind, but I have this comfort, that I have no fault to accuse myself of. This bears me up, and this only. I send you a Paper, in which a letter is fixed for different places, which I may leave at any place, and except those who have the key, none can tell where I am gone to.

July 21st. The Messenger has returned from Cape Passaro, and says, that your letters for me are returned to Naples. What a situation am I placed in! As yet, I can learn nothing of the Enemy; therefore I have no conjecture but that they are gone to Syria and at Cyprus I hope to hear of them. If they were gone to the westward, I rely that every place in Sicily would have information for us, for it is news too important to leave me one moment in doubt about. I have no Frigate, nor a sign of one.   (27)

While Nelson was searching in vain for the enemy, Bonaparte's fleet was slowly approaching Alexandria after its departure from Malta. The following account of his behaviour on board is from the MEMOIRS OF BOURRIENNE, *his secretary.*

On board L'Orient Bonaparte took pleasure in conversing frequently with Monge and Berthollet. The subjects they usually talked about were chemistry, mathematics and religion. General Caffarelli, whose conversation was at once energetic, witty and lively, was one of those with whom he most willingly discoursed. Whatever friendship he might entertain for Berthollet, it was easy to see that he preferred Monge, because Monge, endowed with an ardent imagination, without exactly possessing religious principles, had a kind of predisposition for religious ideas which fell in with the ideas of Bonaparte.

Bonaparte sometimes talked with Admiral Brueys. His object was always to gain information respecting tactics, and nothing astonished the Admiral more than the sagacity of his questions . . .

He passed a great deal of his time in his cabin, lying on a bed which, swinging on a kind of castors, alleviated the severity of the sea sickness, from which he often suffered when the ship rolled. I was almost always with him in his cabin, where I read to him some of his favourite works, which he selected from his camp library . . . His principle was, as he often said to me, to look upon religions as the work of men, but to respect them everywhere as a powerful means of government. I will not go so far as to say that he would have changed his religion, had the conquest of the East been the price. All that he said about Mahomet, Islam and the Koran he laughed at himself. He enjoyed the gratification of having all his fine sayings translated into Arabic and repeated from mouth to mouth. This, of course, tended to conciliate people . . .

The General had a Turkish dress made, which he once put on as a joke. One day he asked me to go to breakfast without waiting for him. In about a quarter of an hour he appeared in his new costume. As soon as he was recognised, he was received with a loud burst of laughter. He sat down, very coolly; but he found himself so ill at ease in his turban and oriental robe that he soon threw them off and was never tempted to assume the disguise. **(28)**

The French reach Aboukir

These letters from Jaubert, the Commissary to the French Fleet, were among those intercepted by British cruisers. The chart referred to is in C. Savary's Lettres sur L'Egypte *(1786), the principal authority on that country at the time. Cleopatra's Needle is now on the Thames Embankment. The first letter from Jaubert to his brother from* L'Orient *off Aboukir is dated 8 July 1798:*

Here we are, my dear Jaubert, on the coasts of Egypt. Our brave troops have already got a footing in its territory, and everything announces that ere long the improvident despotism of the Mamelouks and the apathy of the Egyptians will be succeeded by a creative government and by a spirit of emulation hitherto unknown to its inhabitants.

We are masters of Alexandria. On our march we seized Aboukir and Rosetta and are consequently in possession of one of the principal mouths of the Nile. You may trace our route on the chart to Savary's Voyage, which I suppose you have before you.

At six in the morning of the first instant we were within six leagues of Alexandria. The *Juno* was dispatched to the port with a letter to the French Consul. This was the ostensible motive, but her secret orders were, at all events, to bring him and all the French in the city on board the fleet. Everything there was in confusion. A French invasion had been openly talked of for two months, and measures were taken (as measures usually are taken by the Turks) to prevent it. The appearance of an English squadron of 14 sail on 28 June, and which the Governor had obstinately maintained to be ours, had redoubled the terrors of the city and rendered the situation of the French residents there more and more critical. The Consul, however, obtained permission to go on board the *Juno*, on promising to return in three hours; and the frigate directly put to sea with him. On his arrival on board *L'Orient* the necessity of immediate measures appeared, not only to anticipate the English in getting possession of Alexandria, but to shelter our fleet from an engagement which must be on unequal terms, in the confusion of a first anchorage on unknown ground.

The English fleet has played with ill luck on its side; first it missed us on the coast of Sardinia, next, it missed convoy of 57 sail coming from Civita Vecchia, with 7,000 troops of the army of Italy. It did not arrive at Malta till five days after we had left it; and it arrived at Alexandria two days before we reached it! It is to be presumed that it is gone to Alexandretta with the idea that the army is to be disembarked there for the conquest of India. We shall certainly see it at last, but we are now moored in such a manner as to bid defiance to a force more than double our own . . .

Alexandria is a heap of ruins, where you see a paltry hovel of mud and straw against the magnificent fragments of a granite column. The streets are not paved. This image of desolation is rendered the more striking by being within view of two objects which

London. July 10th 1802. Published by Colnaghi & Co. Cockspur Street

Morizet sculp.

THE OBELISK AT ALEXANDRIA,
generally called CLEOPATRA'S NEEDLE, *as cleared to its base by the* BRITISH TROOPS *in* EGYPT,
and similar to the one laying by it, intended to be brought to ENGLAND.
From the original Drawing by Lt. Col. Monbasor 80th Regt. in the possession of the Right Honorable the Earl of Cavan, then commanding in chief His Majesty's Forces in Egypt.
To whom this plate is by permission respectfully dedicated by His Lordships most obedient humble Servants Colnaghi & Co.

have passed uninjured through the lapse of ages that has devoured everything around them. One is what is called Pompey's Column, but which was raised by Severus; the other which is called Cleopatra's Needle. It is an obelisk formed of a single piece of granite, exceedingly well preserved. As far as I could judge from my eye, it is about 72ft high, 7ft square at the base and 4ft towards the summit; it is covered with hieroglyphics on every side. A few date trees are scattered here and there about the country. Such is the coast of this country, so fertile in the interior! and which, under an enlightened government, might see once more revived the age of Alexander and the Ptolemies . . .

9 July

We are now moored at Aboukir, about five leagues to the east of Alexandria. The road is well enough in summer, but in winter is quite impassable. The English are in our neighbourhood. They have 14 sail, of which 3 are rather old. We are in expectation of them. The general opinion (but this might be influenced in some degree by personal considerations) was that as soon as the debarkation was over, we should have sailed for Corfu, where we were to be reinforced by ships from Malta, Toulon and Ancona, and thus prepared for all events. The General has decided otherwise. The good fortune which attends all his operations will not fail to follow this, and for the rest we are under a gale of fatalism and its breath shakes my principles a little . . .   (29)

While Bonaparte's army marched rapidly inland after its landing at Alexandria, Admiral Brueys anchored his fleet in Aboukir Bay. His LETTER *to Bonaparte dated 13 July 1798 was pessimistic about a conflict:*
I have been taking up a strong position, in case I am compelled to fight at anchor. The work has gone on slowly because of strong northerly winds. I have asked for two mortars from Alexandria to place on the shoal where I have placed the head of my line, but I have less to fear from that part than from the rear, where the enemy is most likely to direct his efforts. This bay is too open for a squadron to take up a tactical position against the attack of a superior enemy.

From our soundings at the Old Port (Alexandria) we hope to find a channel where there is at least $5\frac{1}{2}$ fathoms. If it exists, our ships can enter with a favourable wind and a calm sea, but there is always the question of exit, which would be difficult and dangerous.

Every day I send a boat to the fort at Aboukir and to Rosetta when the wind is not too strong. It would be useful to have a few *djerms* (flat-bottomed boats) for the service of the fleet to fetch water, of which we are in great need, as well as wood to burn. The crews of our ships are very weak, composed of invalid soldiers, young and insubordinate. It seems that in the choice made for your army we were left with the worst.   (30)

The Battle

The following three accounts of the Battle of the Nile describe the event from different points of view. The first is by CAPTAIN BERRY, *Nelsons' flag captain, and was first printed in the* Sun *newspaper. The second is by Midshipman* GEORGE ELLIOTT, *whose ship led the line and had on board the only available chart from Bellini's* Petit Atlas Maritime *of 1764. The last is from the* OFFICIAL LOG *of the* Vanguard.
The Admiral had, and it appeared most justly, the highest opinion of, and placed the firmest reliance on the valour and conduct of every Captain in his Squadron. It had been his practice during the whole of the Cruize, whenever the weather and circumstances would permit, to have his captains on board the *Vanguard*, where he would fully develop to them his own ideas of the different and best modes of

Attack, and such plans as he proposed to execute on falling in with the Enemy, whatever their position or situation might be, by day or night. There was no possible position in which they could be found that he did not take into his calculation, and for the most advantageous attack for which he had not digested and arranged the best possible disposition of the Force which he commanded. With the masterly ideas of their Admiral, on the subject of Naval Tactics, every one of the Captains of his Squadron was most thoroughly acquainted; and upon surveying the situation of the Enemy, they could ascertain with provision what were the ideas and intentions of their Commander, without the aid of further instructions; by which means Signals became almost unnecessary, much time was saved, and the attention of every Captain could almost undisturbably be paid to the conduct of his own particular Ship . . .

The Admiral made the Signal to prepare for Battle, and that it was his intention to attack the Enemy's Van and Centre as they lay at anchor, and according to the plan before developed. His idea of the disposition of his Force was, first to secure the Victory, and then to make the most of it, according to future circumstances. A bower cable of each Ship was immediately got abaft, and bent forward. We continued carrying sail and standing in for the Enemy's Fleet in a close line of Battle. As all Officers of the Squadron were totally unacquainted with Aboukir Bay, each Ship kept sounding as she stood in.

The Enemy appeared to be moored in a strong and compact line of Battle, close in with the shore, their Line describing an obtuse angle in its form, flanked by numerous Gunboats, four Frigates, and

12 *The French at anchor at Aboukir Bay, the ships of the line across the bay, with frigates inshore. Foley in* Goliath *has just crossed the van of the French line.* L'Orient *the French flagship stands out clearly in the centre. From the painting by Pocock*

a Battery of guns and mortars on an island in the Van. This situation of the Enemy seemed to secure to them the most decided advantage, as they had nothing to attend to but their Artillery, in their superior skill in the use of which the French so much pride themselves.

The position of the Enemy presented the most formidable obstacle but the Admiral viewed these with the eye of a Seaman determined on attack; and it instantly struck his eager and penetrating mind, that where there was room for an Enemy's Ship to swing, there was room for one of ours to anchor. No further Signal was necessary than those which had already been made. The Admiral's designs were as fully known to his own squadron, as was his determination to conquer, or perish in the attempt. The *Goliath* and *Zealous* had the honour to lead inside . . .   **(31)**

On August 1, 1798, being in the leading ship (*Goliath*) of the fleet, in which no order of sailing was kept, but each ship got on as fast as she could, by way of gaining time; I, as signal midshipman, was sweeping round the horizon ahead with my glass from the royal yard, when I discovered the French fleet at anchor in Aboukir Bay. The *Zealous* was so close to us that had I hailed the deck they must have heard me; I therefore slid down by the backstay and reported what I had seen. We instantly made the signal, but the under toggle of the upper flag at the main came off in breaking the stop, and the lower flag came down —the compass signal was however clear at the peak, but before we could recover our flag, *Zealous* made the signal for the enemy's fleet; we thus lost the credit of first signalising the enemy, which, as signal midshipman, rather affected me.

Captain Foley guessed the signal would be to form line as most convenient; that is, to get into a line as the ships happened to be at the moment. We were actually first by half the length of a ship; but Captain

Hood of the *Zealous* was very much senior to Captain Foley and was a likely man to make a push for the post of honour. Foley gave orders therefore to have our staysails and studding-sails ready to run up to keep our place, and I fortunately saw the flags under the ship's foresail as they left the deck, so that by the time they reached the royal yard to show over it, our sails were going up, and we got a little more start and took the lead. Hood was annoyed but could not help it . . . Foley stood on and Hood followed him, but the third ship in the line, the *Audacious*, brought to and of course forced the two ships between her and the *Vanguard* to do the same. A gap was thus made between the *Goliath* and the *Zealous* and the rest of the fleet of about seven miles, for we never shortened sail till we were coming to an anchor.

The battle therefore began by only two ships against the whole of the enemy's van, a fine example of determination, more spoken of by the French than in England, where perhaps it may not have been known.

When we were nearly within gunshot, standing as aide-de-camp close to the Captain, I heard him say to the Master that he wished he could get inside of the leading ship of the enemy's line. I immediately looked for the buoy on her anchor, and saw it apparently at the usual distance of a cable's length (200 yards), which I reported. They both looked at it, and agreed there was room to pass between the ship and her anchor; the danger was the ship being close up to the edge of the shoal, and it was decided to do it. The Master then had orders to go forward and drop the anchor the moment he saw it was a ship's breadth inside the French ship, so that we should not actually swing on board her. All this was exactly executed. I also heard Foley say he should not be surprised to find the Frenchman unprepared for action on the inner side—and as we passed her bows I saw he was right, her lower deck guns were not run out, and there was lumber, such as bags and boxes on the upper deck ports, which I reported with no small pleasure. We first fired a broadside into the bow—not a shot could miss at that distance—the *Zealous* did the same; and in less than a quarter of an hour this ship was a perfect wreck, without a mast or a broadside gun to fire . . .

The first ship of the body of the fleet was the *Audacious*. She took up a useless berth between the first and second ships of the enemy's line, both of them being utterly beaten and dismasted; the second ship, the *Theseus*, commanded by as good an officer as we had, Captain Miller, an old companion of ours in the inshore squadron off Cadiz, came inside the French line, as we had, and in passing within ten yards gave us three most hearty cheers which our men returned from their guns pretty well. The French were ordered by their officers to cheer in return, but they made such a lamentable mess of it that the laughter in our ships was distinctly heard in theirs—and one of their captains told me that they could never get their men to stand to their guns afterwards . . .

We were all night trying to save our masts, which were much shattered; and I was so knocked up about three o'clock in the morning that I actually fell asleep in the act of hauling up a shroud hawser. The old boatswain laid me down in his cabin close by and two hours after I was all fresh and right again; but the swelling in my neck from a wound had fixed my head very near my left shoulder, in the position I had slept in, and it remained there for several days, though without pain . . .

Captains in those days found their own charts, and had no means of knowledge how far they were correct but by experience. Captain Foley had a French atlas, which proved quite correct, and we passed the long shoal extending from the island just at a safe distance. Captain Hood had an English chart which proved very incorrect, and had we been running by it we should have both have run on shore close on the spit. Foley's running on with only one ship was also most fortunate. The French captains were all on board their admiral's ship and did not expect us to come in that night; they had sent for their boats to return from the shore, where they were procuring water. The senior officer of the van division, seeing us stand on under all sail, got anxious and sent his own boat to hasten off the boats of his division without waiting to fill with water. She had not got back when we were getting very close, and as his own launch was passing the flagship, half laden with water, he got into her, but she pulled up slowly against the fresh sea breeze and did not reach his ship till we had passed her. I saw him waving his hat and calling to his ship when still at a considerable distance. An officer was leaning against his ensign staff listening; at last this officer ran forward to the poop and down to the quarterdeck. We knew what was coming; and off went their whole broadside but just too late to hit us . . .

L'Orient had nearly demolished two of our 74-gun ships, namely *Bellerophon* and *Majestic*, and would no doubt have done much more serious mischief; but fortunately they had been painting the ship, and with true French carelessness had left the paint oil jars on their middle deck; there had been more than one accidental fire of small consequences, but now the oil running into it, blazed up more furiously, and the *Alexander*, who was close on that side, directed all her fire on the spot. All this we know from those who were saved from *L'Orient* and from the *Alexander* . . .   (32)

Moderate Breezes and clear weather. At 1, saw Alexandria bearing S.E. ½ S. 7 or 8 Leagues. At ¼ past 2, recalled the *Alexander* and *Swiftsure*: ½ past, hauled our wind, unbent the best bower cable, took it out of the Stern-port, and bent it again. At 4, Pharos Tower S.S.W., distant 4 or 5 Leagues: the *Zealous* made the signal for the French Fleet—sixteen Sail of the Line. At 5, bore up for the French

Fleet—sounding 15, 14, 13, 11 and 10 fathoms. At 28 minutes past 6, the French Fleet hoisted their Colours and opened their fire on our Van Ships: ½ past 6, came-to with the best bower in 8 fathoms, veered to half a cable. At 31 minutes past, opened our fire on the *Spartiate*, which was continued without intermission until ½ past 8, when our opponent struck to us. Sent Lieutenant Galwey and a party of Marines to take possession of her. At 9, saw three others strike to the *Zealous*, *Audacious* and *Minotaur*. At 55 minutes past 8 *L'Orient* took fire, the Ships ahead still keeping up a strong fire upon the Enemy. At 10, *L'Orient* blew up with a violent explosion, and the Enemy ceased their fire. 10 minutes past 10, perceived another Ship on fire, which was soon extinguished and a fresh Cannonade began. 20 minutes past 10, a total cease of fire for 10 minutes, when it was again renewed. At 16 minutes past 12, Lieutenant Vassal with a party of Marines, went to take possession of a prize: 15 minutes past 2 (A.M. of the 2nd August) a Boat came from Alexander: 55 minutes past 2, a total cease of firing.

During the course of the action Nelson was wounded in the forehead. This account is by the editor of his despatches, SIR HARRIS NICOLAS. **(33)**

Sir Horatio, for many preceding days, had hardly eaten or slept; but now, with a coolness peculiar to our naval character, he ordered his dinner to be served, during which the dreadful preparations for battle were made throughout the *Vanguard*. On his officers rising from the table and repairing to their separate stations, he exclaimed 'Before this time tomorrow, I shall have gained a Peerage or Westminster Abbey'. It is nowhere stated at what precise time Nelson was wounded; but Captain Berry's

13 *About four hours after the battle began,* L'Orient *blew up. She took to the bottom the treasures of Malta, a mainstay of expedition finances. From the painting by Brown.*

Narrative, compared with the *Vanguard's* log proves that it was before half-past eight in the evening; and his biographers (Clerke and McArthur) say he was at the moment looking over a rough sketch of the Bay of Aboukir, which had been taken out of a French ship by Captain Hallowell a few days before the action, and given by him to the Admiral. He was struck in the forehead by a langridge shot, or a piece of iron, and the skin being cut at right angles, it hung down over his face, and as it covered his eye he was rendered perfectly blind. Captain Berry standing near him, caught him in his arms, and he exclaimed, 'I am killed; remember me to my wife'. On being carried below to the Cockpit, Mr. Jefferson the Surgeon immediately attended him, but he said 'No, I will take my turn with my brave followers'. The pain was intense and Nelson felt convinced that his wound was mortal. Mr. Jefferson assured him, on probing the wound, that there was no immediate danger. He would not, however, indulge any hope, and having desired Mr. Comyn, his Chaplain, to convey his dying remembrance to Lady Nelson, he ordered the *Minotaur* to be hailed, that he might thank her brave and gallant Captain Louis for coming up so nobly to the support of the *Vanguard*; the interview affected all who beheld it. Mr. Jefferson having bound up and dressed the wound, requested the Admiral to remain quiet in the bread-room; but nothing could repress his anxious and enthusiastic disposition. He immediately ordered his Secretary, Mr. Campbell, to attend him in the bread-room, that no time might be lost in writing to the Admiralty. This gentleman, who died soon after, had been himself wounded; and beholding the blind and suffering state of the Admiral, became so much affected, that he could not write. The Chaplain was then summoned; but the eagerness and impatience of Nelson increasing, he took the pen himself; and contrived to trace some words which marked at that awful moment his devout sense of the success he had then obtained.

44

It is then said, He was after this left alone: when, suddenly, the news of the French Admiral's Ship, *L'Orient*, being on fire, re-echoed throughout the decks of the *Vanguard*. Unassisted and unnoticed amidst the general confusion, Nelson contrived to find his way up the ladders, and to the astonishment of every one, appeared again on the quarter-deck'. This, however, is not true. On *L'Orient's* taking fire, Captain Berry went below, to acquaint the Admiral with the circumstances, and he led him upon deck to witness the conflagration. He immediately gave orders that his First Lieutenant Galwey, should be sent in the only boat which the *Vanguard* had saved, with others from his Squadron, to the relief of the Enemy. After the dreadful explosion of *L'Orient* he was persuaded, though with some difficulty to go to bed. (34)

NELSON TO THE CAPTAINS OF HIS SQUADRON *from* Vanguard *off the mouth of the Nile, 2 August 1798:*
Almighty God having blessed His Majesty's Arms with Victory, the Admiral intends returning Public Thanksgiving for the same at two o'clock this day; and he recommends every Ship doing the same as soon as convenient. HORATIO NELSON. (35)

On 3 August Nelson sent this DESPATCH *to St Vincent from* Vanguard *off the mouth of the Nile:*
My Lord, Almighty God has blessed His Majesty's Arms in the late Battle by a great victory over the Fleet of the Enemy, who I attacked at sunset on the 1st August off the Mouth of the Nile. The Enemy were moored in a strong line of Battle for defending the entrance of the Bay, flanked by numerous Gunboats, four Frigates and a Battery of Guns and Mortars on the Island in their Van; but nothing

14 *Sir Thomas Foley from the portrait by Pickersgill. A true follower of Nelson, he crossed the French van without orders and began the battle*

could withstand the Squadron your Lordship did me the honour to place under my command. Their high state of discipline is well known to you and with the judgement of their Captains, together with their Valour and that of the Officers and Men of every description, it was absolutely irresistable. Could anything from my pen add to the character of the Captains, I would write it with pleasure, but that is impossible . . .

The Ships of the Enemy, all but their two rear ships, are nearly dismasted, and those two, with two frigates, I am sorry to say, made their escape; nor was it, I assure you, in my power to prevent them. Captain Hood most handsomely endeavoured to do it, but I had no ship in a condition to support the *Zealous*, and I was obliged to call her in.

The support and assistance I have received from Captain Berry cannot be sufficiently expressed. I was wounded in the head, and obliged to be carried off deck; but the service suffered no loss by that event: Captain Berry was full equal to the important service then going on, and to him I must beg leave to refer you for every information relative to this victory. He will present you with the Flag of the Second in Command, that of the Commander-in-Chief being burnt in *L'Orient*.

Herewith I transmit you Lists of the Killed and Wounded, and the Lines of Battle of ourselves and the French. I have the honour to be, my Lord, your Lordship's obedient Servant, HORATIO NELSON.

LINE OF BATTLE

1. CULLODEN	—T. Troubridge, Captain 74 Guns, 590 Men
2. THESEUS	—R. W. Miller, Captain 74 Guns, 590 Men
3. ALEXANDER	—Alex. John Ball, Captain 74 Guns, 590 Men
4. VANGUARD	—Rear-Admiral Sir Horatio Nelson, K.B., Edward Berry, Captain 74 Guns, 595 Men
5. MINOTAUR	—Thomas Louis, Captain 74 Guns, 640 Men
6. LEANDER	—Thomas B. Thompson, Captain 50 Guns, 343 Men
7. SWIFTSURE	—B. Hallowell, Captain 74 Guns, 590 Men
8. AUDACIOUS	—Davidge Gould, Captain 74 Guns, 590 Men
9. DEFENCE	—John Peyton, Captain 74 Guns, 590 Men
10. ZEALOUS	—Samuel Hood, Captain 74 Guns, 590 Men
11. ORION	—Sir James Saumarez, Captain 74 Guns, 590 Men
12. GOLIATH	—Thomas Foley, Captain 74 Guns, 590 Men
13. MAJESTIC	—George B. Westcott, Captain 74 Guns, 590 Men
14. BELLEROPHON	—Henry D'E Darby, Captain. La Mutine, Brig. 74 Guns, 590 Men

FRENCH LINE OF BATTLE

1. LE GUERRIER	—74 Guns, 700 Men—Taken
2. LE CONQUÉRANT	—74 Guns, 700 Men—Taken
3. LE SPARTIATE	—74 Guns, 700 Men—Taken

4. L'AQUILON	—74 Guns, 700 Men— Taken
5. LE SOUVERAIN PEUPLE	—74 Guns, 700 Men— Taken
6. LE FRANKLIN	—Blanquet, First Contre Amiral, 80 Guns, 800 Men—Taken
7. L'ORIENT	—Brueys, Admiral and Commander-in-Chief, 120 Guns, 1010 Men— Burnt
8. LE TONNANT	—80 Guns, 800 Men— Taken
9. L'HEUREUX	—74 Guns, 700 Men— Taken
10. LE TIMOLEON	—74 Guns, 700 Men— Burnt
11. LE MERCURE	—74 Guns, 700 Men— Taken
12. LE GUILLAUME TELL	—Villeneuve, Second Contre Amiral, 80 Guns, 800 Men—Escaped
13. LE GÉNÉREUX	—74 Guns, 700 Men— Escaped

FRIGATES

14. LA DIANE	—48 Guns, 300 Men— Escaped
15. LA JUSTICE	—44 Guns, 300 Men— Escaped
16. L'ARTEMISE	—36 Guns, 250 Men— Burnt
17. LA SERIEUSE	—36 Guns, 250 Men— Dismasted and Sunk (36)

The following three accounts of the battle are from the French point of view. The first, by ADMIRAL BLANQUET, *describes the loss of* L'Orient, *one of the biggest ships afloat; the second is by* POUSSIELGUE, *Paymaster of the Army, who describes the scene from the land; the third, from* BOURRIENNE'S MEMOIRS, *shows how Bonaparte received the news of the disaster.*

All the van were attacked on both sides by the enemy, who ranged close along our line. They had each an anchor out astern which facilitated their movements and enabled them to place themselves in the most advantageous positions. At a quarter past six, the *Franklin* opened fire upon the enemy from the starboard side: at three-quarters past six she engaged on both sides. The *L'Orient* at the same time began firing her starboard guns and at seven o'clock the *Tonnant* opened fire. All the ships, from the *Guerrier* to the *Tonnant* were now engaged with a superior force: this only redoubled the ardour of the French, who kept up a regular and steady fire. At eight o'clock at night the ship [*Bellerophon*] which engaged *L'Orient* on the starboard quarter, notwithstanding her advantageous position, was dismasted and so roughly treated that she cut her cables and drove far from the line. This event gave the *Franklin* hopes that *L'Orient* would now be able to assist her by attacking one of the ships opposed to her; but at this very moment the two ships which had been seen astern of the fleet [*Swiftsure, Alexander*] and were quite fresh steered right for the centre. One of them anchored on *L'Orient*'s starboard bow and the other cut the line astern of the *L'Orient* and anchored on her larboard quarter. The action in this part then became extremely warm. Admiral Brueys, who at this time had been slightly wounded in the head and arm, very soon received a shot in the belly which almost cut him in two. He desired not to be carried below, but to be left to die upon deck. He only lived a quarter of an hour. Rear-Admiral Blanquet received a severe wound in the face which knocked

him down. He was carried off the deck, senseless. At a quarter past 8, the *Peuple Souverain* drove to leeward of the Line, and anchored a cable's length abreast of *L'Orient*. It was not known what unfortunate event occasioned it. The vacant space she made placed the *Franklin* in a most unfortunate position, and it became very critical, by the manoeuvre of one of the Enemy's fresh Ships [*Leander*], which had been to the assistance of the Ship on shore. She anchored athwart the *Franklin's* bows, and commenced a very heavy raking fire. Notwithstanding the dreadful situation of the Ships in the centre, they continually kept up a very heavy fire.

Those of the officer and Ship's company of *L'Orient* who had escaped death, convinced of the impossibility of extinguishing the fire, which had got down to the middle-gun deck, endeavoured to save themselves. Rear-Admiral Ganteaume saved himself in a boat, and went on board the *Salamine*, and from thence to Aboukir and Alexandria. The Adjutant-General Motard, although badly wounded, swam to the Ship nearest *L'Orient*, which proved to be English. Commodore Casabianca and his son, only ten years old, who during the Action gave proofs of bravery and intelligence far above his age, were not so fortunate. They were in the water, upon the wreck of *L'Orient's* mast, not being able to swim, seeking each other, until three-quarters past 10, when the Ship blew up, and put an end to their hopes and fears. The explosion was dreadful, and spread the fire all round to a considerable distance. The *Franklin's* decks were on fire with red-hot pincers, pieces of timber, and rope. She was on fire the fourth time, but luckily got it under. Immediately after the tremendous explosion, the action ceased everywhere, and was succeeded by the most profound silence.

15 *Poussielgue, financial adviser to the French expedition, who witnessed the Battle of the Nile from the shore. From the drawing by Dutertre*

The sky was obscured by thick clouds of black smoke, which seemed to threaten the destruction of the two Fleets. It was a quarter of an hour before the Ship's crews recovered from the kind of stupor they were thrown into. Towards 11 o'clock, the *Franklin*, anxious to preserve the trust confided to her, recommenced the action with a few of her lower-deck guns; all the rest were dismounted, two-thirds of her Ship's company being killed or wounded, and those who remained much fatigued. She was surrounded by Enemy Ships, some of which were within pistol-shot, and who mowed down the men every broadside. At half-past 11 o'clock, having only three lower-deck guns that could defend the honour of the Flag, it became necessary to put an end to so disproportioned a struggle; and Citizen Martinet, Captain of a Frigate, ordered the Colours to be struck.　　　　　　　　　　　　　(37)

POUSSIELGUE TO HIS WIFE *from Rosetta, 4 August 1798:* We have just been witnesses, my dear girl, of the most bloody and unfortunate naval action that has been fought for many ages. We do not yet know all the circumstances of it, but those that we do know are horrible. The French fleet, composed of 13 sail of the line, of which one was a three-decker of 120 guns, and three of 80, was moored in the incommodious bay of Aboukir, the only station to be found on the coast of Egypt. For the last week several English frigates had frequently reconnoitred the position of our fleet, so that it was in constant expectation of being attacked. From Aboukir to Rosetta is about ten miles, so that from the heights of this latter place our ships were plainly discernible.

The first of this month, at half-past five in the evening, we heard the report of several guns: this was the commencement of the action. We immediately got on to the roofs of the highest houses and clearly distinguished ten English warships, the others not yet in sight. The firing was exceedingly brisk till a quarter after nine, when we saw by favour of the night a prodigious light, which sufficiently told us that some vessel was in flames; at this moment the fire was brisker than ever. At ten o'clock the vessel which was burning blew up with a tremendous noise, which was heard plainly at Rosetta. This accident was succeeded by a pitchy darkness and a most profound silence, which continued for about ten minutes . . .

We drew a very unfavourable augury from this silence; we were compelled, however, to remain in this state of uncertainty all the night of the 2nd. At length, on the morning of the 3rd, a boat, which had slipped out of Alexandria in the night, brought us some details, but of a most melancholy nature. They told us that some of the officers of the French fleet, who had escaped in a shallop to Alexandria, had reported that soon after the commencement of the action Admiral Brueys had received three dangerous wounds, one on the head and two in the body; that he persisted on remaining on the quarterdeck; and that a fourth shot had cut him in two; that his first Captain, Casabianca, had been killed at the same instant by a cannon ball; that the ship was just then perceived to be on fire; that they could not succeed in putting it out; and that she had finally blown up about ten in the evening. They added that our squadron was defeated and destroyed; that four [three] only had escaped; and that the rest were in the enemy's hands.

Nelson commented on this letter that 'this Frenchman seems to know so much more of the battle than I do that I will not venture to contradict him: I am satisfied with it, if he is. Send it to Lady Nelson when read.' In a later letter Poussielgue gives a good summary of the broader results of the battle:

The fatal engagement ruined all our hopes; it prevented us from receiving the remainder of the forces which were destined for us; it left the field free for the English to persuade the Porte to declare war against us; it rekindled that which was barely extinguished in the heart of the Emperor of Austria; it opened the Mediterranean to the Russians and planted them on our frontiers; it occasioned the loss of Italy and the invaluable possessions on the Adriatic which we owed to the successful campaigns of Bonaparte, and finally it rendered abortive all our projects, since it was no longer possible for us to dream of giving the English any uneasiness in India. Added to this was the effect on the people of Egypt, whom we wished to consider as friends and allies. They became our enemies and, entirely surrounded as we were by Turks, we found ourselves engaged in a most difficult defensive war, without a glimpse of the slightest advantage to be obtained from it.

(38)

In spite of assertions to the contrary, the fact is that as soon as the French troops set foot in Egypt they were filled with dissatisfaction and ardently longed to return home. The illusion of the expedition had disappeared and only the reality remained. What bitter murmurings have I not heard from Murat, Lannes, Berthier and others! Their complaints, indeed, often amounted to sedition. This greatly vexed Bonaparte and drew from him severe reproaches in violent language. When the news arrived of the loss of the fleet, discontent increased. All who had acquired fortunes under Bonaparte now began to fear that they would never enjoy them. All turned their thoughts to Paris and its amusements . . .

When alone with me Bonaparte gave free vent to his emotion. I observed that the disaster was doubtless great, but it would have been infinitely greater had Nelson fallen in with us at Malta, or had he waited twenty-four hours for us at Alexandria. Any one of these events would have deprived us of every resource. We are blockaded here, but we have provisions and money. Let us then wait to see what the Directory will do for us. 'The Directory!' he exclaimed, 'the

Directory is composed of a set of scoundrels! They envy and hate me, and would gladly let me perish here. Besides, you see how dissatisfied the whole army is: not a man is willing to stay!' . . .

I drew up for him the draft of a letter for the Directory. After having read it, Bonaparte smiled and returned it to me, saying 'This is too soft; it is not pointed enough. We must enter into more detail, and mention those who have distinguished themselves. Besides, you make it appear that Brueys is blameless. This will not do. You do not know the men we have to deal with. I will tell you what to write'. He then dictated to me a despatch. (39)

A Lower Deck View of the Battle

From THE LIFE AND ADVENTURES OF JOHN NICOL, MARINER, *dictated in his old age and printed in 1822:*
The sun was just setting as we went into the bay, and a red and fiery sun it was. I would, if I had my choice, have been on the deck; there I would have seen what was passing, and the time would not have hung so heavily; but every man does his duty with spirit, whether his station be in the slaughter-house or the magazine. I saw as little of this action as I did of the one of the 14 February off Cape St Vincent. My station was in the powder magazine with the gunner. As we entered the bay, we stripped to our trousers, opened our ports, cleared and every ship we passed gave them a broadside and three cheers. Any information we got was from the boys and women who carried the powder. The women behaved as well as the men, and got a present for their bravery from the Grand Signior. When the French Admiral's ship blew up, the *Goliath* got such a shake we thought the after-part of her had blown up, until the boys told us what it was. They brought us every now and then the cheering news of another French ship having struck, and we answered the cheers on deck with heart-felt joy. In the heat of the action, a shot came right into the magazine, but did no harm as the carpenters plugged it up and stopped the water rushing in. I was much indebted to the gunner's wife, who gave her husband and me a drink of wine every now and then, which lessened our fatigue much. There were some of the women wounded and one woman belonging to Leith died of her wounds and was buried on a small island in the bay. One woman bore a son in the heat of the action; she belonged to Edinburgh. When we ceased firing I went on deck to see the state of the fleets, and an awful sight it was. The whole bay was covered with dead bodies, mangled, wounded and scorched, not a bit of clothes on them except their trousers. There were a number of the French belonging to the *L'Orient* who had swum to the *Goliath* and were cowering under her forecastle. Poor fellows, they were brought on board and Captain Foley ordered them down to the steward's room to get provisions and clothing.

The only incidents I heard of were two. One lad who was stationed by a salt-box on which he sat to give out cartridges and keep the lid closed, when asked for a cartridge, he gave none, yet he sat upright: his eyes were open. One of the men gave him a push; he fell all his length on the deck. There was not a blemish on his body, yet he was quite dead and was thrown overboard. The other, a lad who had the match in his hand to fire a gun. In the act of applying it, a shot took off his arm; it hung by a small piece of skin. The match fell to the deck. He looked to his arm, and seeing what had happened, seized the match in his left hand and fired off the gun before he went to the cockpit to have it dressed. They were in our mess, or I might never have heard of it. Thus terminated the glorious first of August, the busiest night in my life. (40)

The Victor Proclaimed

Perhaps the best-known consequence of Nelson's victory was his affair with Lady Hamilton, who nursed him back to health at Palermo. This LETTER TO LADY

NELSON *dated 16 September 1798 illustrates his pride in the first of his victories and the theatrical reception which he had in Sicily.*

The Kingdom of the Two Sicilies is mad with joy; from the throne to the peasant, all are alike. According to Lady Hamilton's letter, the situation of the Queen was truly pitiable: I only hope I shall not have to be a witness to a renewal of it. I give you Lady Hamilton's own words: 'How shall I describe the transports of the Queen? 'tis not possible: she cried, kissed her husband, her children, walked frantic about the room, cried, kissed and embraced every person near her; exclaiming, O brave Nelson! O God bless and protect our brave deliverer. O Nelson, Nelson! what do we not owe you! O Victor! Saviour of Italy! O that my swollen heart could now tell him personally what we owe him!' You may judge, Fanny, of the rest: but my head will not allow me to tell you half; so much for that. My fag, without success, would have had no effect, but blessed be God for his goodness to me. Yours etc. HORATIO NELSON.
(41)

The deep affection which Nelson's brother officers had for him is shown in these two letters, the first from Captain Collingwood, who was not at the battle, the second from Captain Hallowell, which accompanied the strange gift of a coffin in which Nelson was ultimately buried.

COLLINGWOOD'S LETTER TO NELSON *from Cadiz on 27 September 1798:*

My dear Friend, I cannot express how great my joy is for the complete and glorious victory you have obtained over the French—the most decisive, and, in its consequence, perhaps the most important to Europe that ever was won. And my heart overflows

16 *Prayers aboard one of HM ships after the battle from the engraving by Atkinson*

with thankfulness to the Divine Providence for his protection of you through the great dangers which are ever attendant on services of such eminence. So total an overthrow of their fleet and the consequent deplorable situation of the army they have in Africa, I hope will teach those tyrants in the Directory a lesson of humility and dispose them to peace and to justice, that they may restore to those states they have ruined all that can be saved out of the wreck of a subverted government and plundered people . . . Say to Lady Nelson when you write to her how much I congratulate her on the safety, the honours and the services of her husband. Good God, what must be her feelings! how great her gratitude to Heaven for such mercies! Pray, my dear Sir, give my hearty congratulations to all my friends in your fleet. May success ever attend you, my dear friend, is ever the prayer of, my dear Sir, your faithful and affectionate, Cuthbert Collingwood. **(42)**

HALLOWELL TO NELSON:
My Lord, Herewith I send you a Coffin made of part of *L'Orient's* main mast, that when you are tired of life you may be buried in one of your own trophies— but may that period be far distant, is the sincere wish of your obedient and much obliged servant. BEN HALLOWELL. **(43)**

The pleasure with which the news was reported in England is illustrated by this ecstatic letter from the wife of the First Lord of the Admiralty, followed by the congratulations of Admiral Lord Howe, to whom Nelson replied in a notable letter.
COUNTESS SPENCER TO NELSON, *2 October 1798:*
Joy, joy, joy to you, brave, gallant, immortalised Nelson! May that great God, whose cause you so valiantly support, protect and bless you to the end of your brilliant career! Such a race surely was never run. My heart is absolutely bursting with different sensations of joy, of gratitude, of pride, of every emotion that ever warmed the bosom of a British woman, on hearing of her Country's glory—and all produced by you, me dear, my good friend . . . But I am come to the end of my paper, luckily for you, or I should gallop on for ever at this rate. I am half mad, and I fear I have written a strange letter, but you'll excuse it. Almighty God protect you! **(44)**

NELSON TO HOWE *from Palermo, 8 January 1799:*
My Lord, It was only this moment that I had the invaluable approbation of the great, the immortal Earl Howe—an honour the most flattering a sea-officer could receive, as it comes from the first and greatest sea-officer the world has ever produced. I had the happiness to command a band of brothers; therefore, night was to my advantage. Each knew his duty, and I was sure that each would feel for a French ship. By attacking the enemy's van and centre, the wind blowing directly along their line, I was enabled to throw what force I pleased on a few ships. This plan my friends readily conceived by the signals (for which we are principally indebted to your Lordship) and we always kept a superior force to the enemy. At twenty-eight minutes past six, the sun in the horizon, the firing commenced. At five minutes past ten, when *L'Orient* blew up, having burnt seventy minutes, the six van ships had surrendered. I then pressed further towards the rear; and had it not pleased God that I had been wounded and stone blind, there cannot be any doubt but that every ship would have been in our possession. But here let it not be supposed that any officer is to blame. No; on my honour, I am satisfied that each did his very best. I have never before, my Lord, detailed the action, but I should have thought it very wrong to have kept it from one who is our great master in naval tactics and bravery. May I presume to present my very best respects to Lady Howe, and to Lady Mary; and to beg that your Lordship will believe me ever your most obliged, NELSON. **(45)**

Nelson's Account of the Approach to the Battle of the Nile

Lord Fitzharris, son of the Earl of Malmesbury, one of Britain's ambassadors, met Nelson at Vienna in 1799, when Nelson told him the following story:

When I saw them (the French ships) I could not help popping my head every now out of the window, although I had a damned toothache, and once when I was observing their position I heard two seamen quartered at a gun near me, talking, and one said to the other 'Damn them, look at them, there they are, Jack, and if we don't beat them, they will beat us.' I knew what stuff I had under me, so I went into the attack with only a few ships, perfectly sure that the others would follow me, although it was nearly dark and they might have had every excuse for not doing it, yet they all in the course of two hours found a hole to poke in at. If I had taken a fleet of the same force from Spithead, I would sooner have thought of flying than attacking the French in their position; but I knew my captains, nor could I say which distinguished himself most. **(46)**

CHAPTER THREE

THE CONQUEST OF EGYPT (1798-9)

On 1 July 1798, the French army landed on the Marabut beach west of Alexandria. Within forty-eight hours the city had fallen into its hands. Two days later divisions of some 18,000 men were sent to occupy Rosetta and Damanhur, the chief towns of the western part of the delta, while Brueys anchored the fleet in Aboukir Bay on 7 July. The flying columns and the main body of the army were to unite at El Rahmaniya on the Nile on 11 July.

Immediately on landing, Bonaparte issued proclamations to the Turks and to the inhabitants of Egypt in an unavailing attempt to set them against the Mameluke Beys, who were the real rulers of the country. For five centuries these warriors of Georgian and Caucasian stock had ruled this outlying province of the Ottoman Empire. The word 'mameluke' means in Arabic 'bought man': they were not exactly slaves, but boys recruited from the area of the Caucasus to be trained as a military caste numbering about 10,000 soldiers. Though nominally owing allegiance to the Sultan, their chieftains or Beys were the effective rulers of Egypt. They kept themselves apart from the subservient inhabitants of the Nile valley. Knowing no master except his Bey, and having no settled habitation, every Mameluke carried all his weapons—pistols, javelins, scimitars—and all his personal possessions on horseback. Like their Cossack ancestors, they were the finest cavalry in the world.

The reason for Bonaparte's rapid advance inland was that he intended to defeat the Mameluke leader, Mourad Bey, before his own army was demoralised by the hardships of the march across the desert. After the delights of Italy, and after all they had been told about the fertility and riches of Egypt, their experiences in the desert until they reached the Nile were enough to disillusion the most dedicated soldier. They were accompanied by a flotilla of boats up the Nile, and it was the stiff opposition which this flotilla encountered in the river craft manned by Mamelukes which prevented Bonaparte from decisively defeating the enemy at the first encounter.

This was at the Battle of Shubra Kit, eight miles south of El Rahmaniya on 14 July. When the Mamelukes attacked in their usual style of massed cavalry charges, the French formed squares and met them with a hail of artillery and musketry fire. After an hour of unvailing attempts to break the squares, the Mamelukes withdrew to the south and Bonaparte was able to extricate his flotilla from its fight with the enemy on the river.

A week later, on 21 July, the decisive battle was fought at Embaba, known to history as the Battle of the Pyramids, because it was fought ten miles from the Great Pyramid and about twelve north-west of Cairo. The main force of the enemy was on the left bank of the Nile, with a reserve under Ibrahim Bey on the right bank. The battle began in the middle of the afternoon during the worst heat of the day, with 25,000 Frenchmen opposed by a force which Bonaparte estimated at 12,000 Mamelukes (each with two or three servants), 8,000 Bedouin and 20,000 janissaries or foot soldiers, quite apart from Ibrahim's force. Such was the discipline and tactics of the French, which forced the remnants of Mourad's army to escape to Upper Egypt, that there is no need to exaggerate the numbers of the enemy, as Bonaparte seems to have done. Ibrahim's host, blinded by a sandstorm and realising that Mourad had been defeated, withdrew to Cairo and thence took refuge in the desert of Sinai.

The same night Bonaparte established his headquarters in Mourad's house at Giza, where he received the surrender of Cairo the next day. The entry into the capital was victorious, but the sight of the city which was supposed to be the cradle of civilisation was enough to depress the most optimistic. It was a poverty-stricken conglomeration of hovels, from which rose the majestic minarets, notably those of the centre of Egyptian culture, the mosque of El Azhar. Bonaparte did his best to pacify the Moslem inhabitants by fraternising with the scholars and priests and ruling through the notables, while at the same time trying to improve the morale of his army by asking the Directory to send troupes of ballet dancers, theatrical companies, doctors, gardeners etc, to Egypt. Needless to say, none arrived. More important was his introduction of the first printing press, with three sets of type in Arabic, Greek and French for propaganda purposes, and his establishment of the Institute of Egypt under Monge. The ten volumes of its Description of Egypt, with its fourteen volumes of plates, form the monument of its three years of work.

The defeat of the remaining Mameluke forces was Bonaparte's first requirement. General Belliard was sent 150 miles across the desert to seize Kosseir, near Suez, which he succeeded in doing although most of his army was already suffering from opthalmia, the curse of Egypt. General Desaix was sent to bring Mourad to battle in Upper Egypt. Though he got as far as Aswan he never succeeded in coming to grips with the highly mobile Mameluke force. In Cairo itself an uneasy acquiescence in French rule lasted for a few months until the city rose in revolt on 21 October. The rebellion was immediately suppressed. 'Many people were killed, and their corpses thrown into the Nile', wrote the chronicler El Djabarti. 'Only God knows how many died during these few days.'

As the year drew to a close, two more serious threats to French rule developed. Outbreaks of plague were reported in both Alexandria and Cairo, and Bonaparte heard the news that the Ottoman Porte had declared war against him. At first he refused to believe it, assuring the Turks that he had no quarrel with them and warning the Pasha of Syria of the consequences of collecting an army. These efforts to allow himself time to organise the French Rule in Egypt had no effect, so that early in the new year he was compelled to undertake the Syrian campaign.

Mameluck chargeant l'Ennemi. (N.º 9) *A Mameluke charging the Ennemy.*

Déposé à la Bibliothèque Impériale. à Paris, chez Bulver Rue ...

ORDER OF THE DAY *to the Army of the East from* L'Orient, *28 June, 1798:*

Soldiers!

You are going to undertake a conquest whose effects on civilisation and the commerce of the world will be incalculable.

You will strike the surest and most painful stroke

17 *A contemporary print of a Mameluke horseman in action after a drawing by Vernet*

possible against England until you can deal her final death-blow.

We shall undergo tiring marches; we shall fight several battles; we shall succeed in all our enterprises; Destiny is with us.

58

The Mameluke beys, who favour English trade exclusively, who have covered our merchants with insults and tyrannize over the unfortunate inhabitants of the Nile, will have ceased to exist a few days after our arrival.

The people amongst whom we are going to live are Mohammedans; the first article of their faith is: 'There is no other God but God, and Mahomet is his prophet.'

Do not argue with them; behave towards them as we behaved towards the Jews and the Italians; show respect to their muftis and imams as you have to rabbis and bishops.

Have for the mosques and the ceremonies prescribed by the Koran the same tolerance that you showed for convents and synagogues, for the religion of Moses and of Jesus Christ.

The Roman legions protected all religions. You will find here customs different from those of Europe; you must get used to them.

The people amongst whom we are going treat women differently from us; but, in every country, he who commits rape is a monster.

Pillage enriches but a few; it dishonours us, it destroys our resources, it makes enemies of the people it is to our interest to have as friends.

The first city we are going to meet was built by Alexander. At each step we shall find memories worthy to excite emulation. **(47)**

The Taking of Alexandria

The French landed at Marabut on 1 July and captured Alexandria the next day. This PROCLAMATION *was printed in Arabic, Turkish and French, the Arabic version making a stronger religious appeal . . . At St Helena, Napoleon called it 'charlatanry of the highest sort'.*

TO THE PEOPLE OF EGYPT H.Q. Alexandria 2 July 1798:

The beys who govern Egypt have for long insulted the French nation and injured its merchants: the hour of their punishment has arrived.

For too long this rabble of slaves bought in Georgia and Caucasia have tyrannized over the most beautiful part of the world; but God, from whom all depends, has ordered that their empire shall cease.

Peoples of Egypt, you will be told that I have come to destroy your religion; do not believe it! Answer that I have come to restore your rights and punish the usurpers, and that, more than the Mamelukes, I respect God, his prophet and the Koran.

Say that all men are equal before God; wisdom, talent and virtue alone differentiate between them. But what wisdom, what talents, what virtue have the Mamelukes, that they exclusively have all that makes life desirable and sweet? Is there a fine estate? It belongs to the Mamelukes. Is there a beautiful slave, a good horse, a pleasant house? They belong to the Mamelukes.

If Egypt is their farm, let them show the lease that God has given them. But God is just and merciful to the people.

The Egyptians will be called upon to hold all offices; the wisest and most learned and most virtuous will govern, and the people will be happy.

Once there were among you great cities, great canals, a great commerce. What has destroyed all this if not greed, the injustice and the tyranny of the Mamelukes?

Cadis, sheiks, imams, tell the people that we are friends of the true Moslems [Arabic text — 'are true Moslems'].

Is it not we who have destroyed the Pope, who called for war against the Moslems? Is it not we who have destroyed the knights of Malta because those madmen believed God wished them to fight the Moslems? Is it not we who have been through the centuries the friends of the Sultan (may God grant his desires) and the enemies of his enemies? But, as for the Mamelukes, have they not ever been

59

in revolt against the Sultan's authority, which even now they disown?

Thrice happy those who shall be for us! They will prosper both in fortune and in rank. Happy those who shall be neutral! They will have time to learn to know us, and they will range themselves beside us.

But woe, threefold woe to those who take up arms for the Mamelukes and fight against us! For them there will be no hope: they will perish.   (48)

BONAPARTE'S REPORT TO THE DIRECTORY *from Alexandria, 6 July 1798.*

The Army left Malta on 1 Messidor (19 June) and arrived before Alexandria at dawn on the 13th (30 June). An English squadron said to be very powerful, had put in there three days earlier and left mails for India . . .

The wind was strong and there was a heavy swell; however, I thought it right to disembark at once. The day was passed in preparing for the landing. General Menou at the head of his division, was the first ashore, near the Marabout, a league and a half from Alexandria.

I landed with General Kléber and another part of the troops at 11 p.m. We at once marched towards Alexandria. At first light we could see Pompey's column. A force of Mamelukes and Arabs began to skirmish with our forward troops; but we moved rapidly on to different parts of Alexandria, General Bon's division being on the right, General Kléber's in the centre, General Menou's on the left. The wall of the Arab city was heavily manned.

General Kléber left Pompey's column to scale the wall, while General Bon forced the Rosetta gate and General Menou, blocking the triangular castle with part of his division, with the rest stormed another part of the wall; he was the first to enter the city. He received seven wounds, but happily none of them were dangerous.

While at the foot of the wall showing his grenadiers where to mount, General Kléber received a bullet in the face, which threw him to the ground. His wound, although extremely grave, is not mortal. At that the grenadiers of his division redoubled their courage and broke into the city . . .

Once we were masters of the Arab city the enemy retired into the triangular fort, the lighthouse and the new city. Every house became a citadel for them. But before the end of the day the city was quiet, the two castles surrendered, and we found ourselves completely masters of the city, the forts and the two harbours of Alexandria.

Meanwhile the Arabs of the desert [Bedouin] had ridden up in groups of thirty to fifty horsemen, attacking our rear and falling upon our stragglers. They did not cease harassing us for two days; but yesterday I succeeded in concluding a treaty, not only of friendship, but even of alliance. Thirteen of the principal chiefs came to my quarters. I sat in the midst of them and we had a very long conversation. After agreeing upon terms we assembled round a table and consigned to hellfire whoever of ours or theirs should break our agreements. These are: on their side, to cease harassing my rear, to give me all the help in their power and to provide the men I ask for to march against the Mamelukes; on mine, to restore them, once I am master of Egypt, the lands which formerly belonged to them.

Prayers are held as usual in the mosques, and my house is always full of imams, cadis, sherifs, chiefs, muftis or religious leaders . . .

This country is not at all inferior to the picture painted by travellers: it is calm, proud and brave . . .

The fleet will be at Aboukir today to finish landing our artillery. The old port of Alexandria can contain a fleet of any size. But there is one point in the passage with only five fathoms of water, which makes the sailors think it impossible for 74s to enter. This fact seriously interferes with my plans.

18 *General Menou from a drawing by Dutertre*

61

19 *The Battle of the Pyramids, a decisive French victory.*
From the painting by Leyenne

At the capture of Alexandria we had 30 to 40 men killed and 80 to 100 wounded [later he admitted to 300 killed].   **(49)**

The Battle of the Pyramids

One column marched to Damanhur, another to Rosetta, uniting at El Rahmaniya on the Nile with a flotilla of boats. The Battle of Shubra Kit was fought eight miles south, and at Embaba, twelve miles from Cairo, Mourad was totally routed at the Battle of the Pyramids, so called from the fact that the Great Pyramid lay ten miles south. The following accounts include Bonaparte's official despatch, a description of the battle by an infantry captain, Vertray, and a personal letter from General Damas showing that the morale of the army was deteriorating in spite of its victories.

BONAPARTE'S OFFICIAL DESPATCH TO THE DIRECTORY *from Cairo, 24 July 1798.*

Citizen Directors, The Army left Alexandria on 19 Messidor (3 July); it reached Damanhur on the 20th, suffering much across the desert from the excessive heat and the lack of water. On the 22nd we met the Nile at El Rahmaniya and rejoined General Dugua's division, which had come by Rosetta . . .

I learned that Murad Bey, at the head of his army composed of a great quantity of cavalry, awaited us at the village of Chobrakhyt (Shubra Kit), with eight or ten gunboats and several batteries on the Nile. On the evening of the 24th we began to march towards them; at dawn on the 25th (July 14) we were in presence. We had only 20 cavalry, still lame and worn out by the crossing. The Mamelukes had a magnificent force of horsemen, covered in gold and silver, armed with the best carbines and pistols of London and the best sabres of the East and mounted on perhaps the best horses of the continent.

The Army was drawn up; the divisions formed in battalion squares with the baggage in the midst and the artillery in the intervals between the squares . . .

Soon the Mameluke cavalry covered the whole plain, outflanked our wings and sought everywhere, on our flanks and rear, for a weak point to penetrate; but it found that the line was always equally formidable and met it with a cross-fire from front and flank. Several times they attempted to charge, but without pressing home. A few braves advanced to skirmish; they were received by the fire of squads of carabiniers placed ahead of the battalion intervals. Finally, after remaining at half cannon range for part of the day, they retreated and disappeared. Their losses can be reckoned at 300 men killed or wounded.

We marched for eight days, deprived of everything and in one of the most burning climates in the world. On the morning of 2 Thermidor (20 July) we saw the Pyramids. In the evening we were six leagues from Cairo, and I learned that the twenty-three beys, with all their forces, were entrenched at Embaba, and that they had mounted more than 60 guns on their parapets.

At first light on the 3rd we encountered their advance guard, while we pushed from village to village. At 2 p.m. we were face to face with the enemy's army and emplacements.

I ordered the divisions of General Desaix and Reynier to take up position on the right, so as to cut the enemy's communication with Upper Egypt, which was his natural retreat. The army was drawn up in the same manner as at the battle of Shubra Kit. As soon as Murad Bey saw General Desaix's movement he decided to charge him. He sent one of his bravest beys with a corps d'élite which charged the two divisions with the speed of lightning. It was allowed to approach within fifty paces and was then welcomed with a hail of case shot and bullets which felled a great many on the field of battle. They threw themselves into the space between the two divisions, where they were met with a double fire which completed their defeat.

I seized that moment and ordered General Bon's division, which was on the Nile, to go in to attack the fortifications, and General Vial to move between the force which had just charged and the emplacements, so as to complete the threefold aim of preventing that force from entering, cutting off the retreat of the force within and, if necessary, of attacking the emplacements from the left . . .

The Mameluke cavalry showed great bravery; they were defending their fortune, and there is not one of them on whom our soldiers have not found 300, 400 or 500 louis of gold. All the wealth of these people was in their horses and arms; their houses are pitiable. It is hard to imagine a land more fertile and a people more wretched, ignorant and brutish. They prefer one of our soldier's buttons to a five-franc piece. In the villages they do not even know of a pair of scissors. Their houses are just mud. For furniture they have only a straw mat and two or three earthenware pots. They generally eat and drink very little. They do not use mills, so that we have constantly bivouacked on great heaps of corn unable to have flour. We feed on vegetables and cattle.   **(50)**

CAPTAIN VERTRAY'S DESCRIPTION OF THE BATTLE

We marched to Embaba, where the Mamelukes waited to give battle, as well as at Gizeh. We arrived very near the Pyramids of Gizeh, which we had already seen for the last three days. I learned some days afterwards that these gigantic constructions were the tombs of the ancient Pharaohs. It was there that Bonaparte pronounced before the battle the famous words—'Soldiers! From the summit of these Pyramids forty centuries look down upon you!'

An hour had scarcely passed since we had taken up our position when we saw the Mamelukes leave their camps by groups, marching with an air of confidence to meet us. The division to which I belonged, and which formed the extreme right, had the honour of being the first attacked. On our front, within gunshot, a small ravine protected the square. When the Mamelukes gained the ditch, which was not deep, General Reynier gave the command 'To your ranks!' and in the twinkling of an eye we were formed in square six men deep, ready to sustain the shock. This movement had been carried out with really remarkable precision and coolness. Scarcely had the order to commence firing been given, when a cloud of cavalry surrounded us. The file firing was so well directed that the charge against our battalion was broken. The Mamelukes hurled themselves against troops that had not their equal, broken to all kinds of fatigues and to all manoeuvres of war, endowed with a coolness and courage proof against anything . . .

Half this splendid army threw itself into the Nile, hoping to be saved by swimming, but we saw the unfortunate wretches swallowed up by thousands in the river; others were taken prisoner, and a band of brave ones alone succeeded in reaching Upper Egypt, following Mourad Bey . . .

The luxury of the Mamelukes was great: they all wore muslin under their shirts and silk pelisses. As for their arms, they were encrusted with ivory and precious stones. They were armed to the teeth, and carried four or five pistols in their belts. Their curved sabres cut like razors and cut off the head at a blow. It was only troops like ours that could resist the formidable charges of the enemy. The demibrigades were composed of old soldiers, accustomed to success; besides, we knew that having no line of retreat we must conquer or die.   **(51)**

GENERAL DAMAS TO GENERAL KLEBER *from Cairo, 27 July 1798.*

We arrived at length, my friend, at the spot so much and so eagerly desired! How different it is from what the most cool and temperate imagination had figured it to be! This execrable doghole of a city is inhabited by a lazy set of wretches, who squat all day before their filthy huts, smoking and taking coffee, or eating pumpkins and drinking water. It is easy to lose oneself for a whole day in the stinking narrow streets of this illustrious capital. The quarter of the

Mamelukes is the only one which is habitable; the Commander-in-Chief resides there in a tolerably handsome house, which belonged to one of the Beys . . .

You have no idea of the fatiguing marches we made to get to Cairo, never halting till three or four o'clock in the afternoon, after broiling in the sun all day; the greatest part of the time without food, obliged to glean what the divisions which preceded us had left in those detestable villages, which they had frequently pillaged; and harassed during the whole march by those hordes of robbers called Bedouins, who killed not only our men but our officers at twenty-five yards from the main body. It is a more destructive war, on my soul, than that of La Vendée!

I very much want to know how you are and when you think you will be able to come and take command of the division, which is in very feeble hands. Everyone wants you here. There is a general relaxation in the service; I do all I can to preserve unity among the different parties, but all goes very ill. The troops are neither paid nor fed, and you may easily guess what murmurs this occasions, loudest perhaps among the officers. We are cajoled with promises that in a week's time the administration will be sufficiently organised to enable them to make distributions regularly, but a week is too long. **(52)**

The French in Cairo

BONAPARTE'S PROCLAMATION TO THE PEOPLE OF CAIRO *from H.Q. Giza 22 July 1798:*
People of Cairo, I am satisfied with your conduct. You have done well not to take sides against me. I have come to destroy the race of Mamelukes and to protect trade and the natives of the country.

Let those who are afraid be calm; those who have fled return to their houses. Let prayers be held today as usual, as I wish them always to be. Fear nothing for your families, your houses, your property, and,

above all, for the religion of the Prophet, whom I love.

Since it is important that the peace be not disturbed, there will be a divan of seven persons which will meet at the Mosque of El-Azhar. There will always be two members attached to the commandant of the city and four will be occupied in maintaining public order and supervising the police. BONAPARTE.

(53)

Bonaparte had hardly conquered Egypt when news reached him of his wife's infidelity in France. He consoled himself with Pauline Fouré, the wife of a lieutenant who was conveniently sent on leave. The first document is a LETTER to his brother, Joseph, dated 25 July. The second is Bourrienne's account of how he heard the news, written some time after the event.
You will see in the public papers the result of our battles and the conquest of Egypt, which met enough resistance to add a page to the military glory of the army. Egypt is the richest country on earth in corn, rice, vegetables, meat. It is utterly barbarous. There is no money, not even enough to pay the troops. In two months I may be back in France. Please look after my interests. I have great private unhappiness; the veil has at last quite fallen from my eyes. Your friendship is very dear to me. It is a sad state to be in to have all one's thoughts centred in the heart of one person.

Arrange for me to have a country house when I get back, either near Paris or in Burgundy; I intend to shut myself up there for the winter; I have had enough of human nature. I need solitude and quiet; grandeur bores me; my emotions are dried up. Glory is stale at twenty-nine; I have used everything up; it only remains for me to become a real egoist. I shall keep my town house; never will I give that up to anyone. I have only enough to live on. Good-bye, my one friend. I have never wronged you. You owe me that at least, whatever my heart may have desired; you understand? Kiss your wife, and Jerome. **(54)**

Whilst near the walls of Messodiah on our way to El Arish I one day saw Bonaparte walking alone with Junot, as he often did. I stood at a little distance and watched him. His face, which was always pale, had, I knew not why, become paler than usual. There was something wild in his look, and he several times struck his head with his hand. After talking to Junot about a quarter of an hour, he left him and came towards me. I never saw him so worried. As soon as he met me he exclaimed angrily 'So! I find I cannot depend on you—these women!—Josephine!—if you had loved me, you would have told me all that I have just heard from Junot before now—he is a real friend—Josephine!—and I am six hundred leagues from her—you ought to have told me—that she should have deceived me! Woe to them! I will exterminate the whole race of fops and puppies— As to her, divorce!—yes, divorce, a public and open divorce! I must write! I know all! It is your fault, you ought to have told me'.

I saw that Junot had been drawn into a culpable indiscretion and that if Josephine had committed any faults, he had cruelly exaggerated them. My situation was one of extreme delicacy . . . I begged Bonaparte to consider how easily stories were fabricated and circulated. I spoke of his glory. 'My glory!' he cried, 'I know not what I would give if that which Junot has told me should be untrue; so much do I love Josephine!' **(55)**

The French were not impressed by Cairo. The first description of the city is by Major Detroye, the second by one of the savants. This was intercepted by the British and printed for propaganda purposes.

Once you enter Cairo, what do you find? Narrow, unpaved and dirty streets, dark houses that are falling to pieces, public buildings that look like dungeons, shops that look like stables, an atmosphere redolent of dust and garbage, blind men, half-blind men, bearded men, people dressed in rags, pressed together in the streets or squatting, smoking their pipes, like monkeys at the entrance of their cave; a few women of the people, hideous, disgusting, hiding their fleshless faces under stinking rags, and displaying their pendulous breasts through their torn gowns; yellow, skinny children covered with suppuration, devoured by flies; an unbearable stench, due to the dirt in the houses, the dust in the air, and the smell of food being fried in bad oil in the un-ventilated bazaars. When you have finished sight-seeing, you return to your house. No comfort, not a single convenience. Flies, mosquitoes, a thousand insects are waiting to take possession of you during the night. Bathed in sweat, exhausted, you spend the hours devoted to rest itching and breaking out in boils. You rise in the morning, unutterably sick, bleary-eyed, queasy in the stomach, with a bad taste in your mouth, your body covered with pimples, or rather ulcers. Another day begins, the exact copy of the preceding one. **(56)**

Grand Cairo, 15 August 1798:
You will see, Citizen Miot, by the date of this letter that it is written twenty days after that which you will find in the same packet. You will see, too, by the conclusion of the former that I was on the point of setting out with General Le Clerc on a secret expedi-tion, the object of which, as I afterwards learned, was to seize the caravan to Mecca, of which Ibrahim Bey had possessed himself. This expedition has totally failed, and we are returned with the loss of a number of our new mounted hussars.

You will easily discover from this wretched scrawl of a letter that something has happened to prevent me from writing as usual. I will tell you briefly (to save unnecessary alarm) that this expedition had been a little, and more than a little, unfortunate for me, since I have had my left arm so torn and bruised by a camel that I shall not be able to use it for a month; there is, however, no danger. By a second accident I had two of my right-hand fingers so much injured as to be scarcely able to hold a pen.

I lost, besides, everything I took with me, except the shirt on my back, Luckily my portmanteau had reached Cairo, so that I shall not be in want of necessaries. I support my misfortunes, which are after all not of the most important nature, in a very philosophical style; the greatest of them all is, however, and always will be, the not having it in my power to see you and press you to my heart. It was at Sallich, just beyond Bilbis, the last village before you come to the desert, that we first heard the melancholy news of our naval action, in which we lost a great number of vessels, and amongst the rest *L'Orient*; and had Admiral Brueys killed by a cannon shot. You may easily conceive how embarrassing this event must render our situation in this country. It would deprive the army of every hope, if they were not acquainted with the genius of the Commander-in-Chief. It is entirely on him, therefore, that we rely for the care of extricating us from the perilous step in which we are engaged. May the measures he may take bring us nearer to our country! EGYPT IS NOT MADE FOR US.

(57)

The Institute of Egypt

Meanwhile the reorganisation of Egypt was carried out by DECREES *and the Institute of Egypt was founded. One of the many inhabitants who visited it was the chronicler El Djabarti and its field workers made important archaeological discoveries, notably the Rosetta Stone.*

H.Q. Cairo, 27 July 1798:

Bonaparte, Member of the National Institute, Commander-in-Chief, orders: Article 1: In each province of Egypt there will be a divan of seven members charged with watching over the interests of the province, informing me of all complaints, preventing war between the villages, supervising

20 *Gillray's cartoon satirising the Institute of Egypt*

"*L'Insurrection de l'Institut A*

SUR
L'EDUCA-
-TION DU
CROCODILE

Etched by J.ˢ Gillray, from the Original Intercepted Drawing.

Pubᵈ March 12ᵗʰ 1799, by H.Humphrey S.ᵗ James's Street.

The Pursuit of Knowledge

and punishing criminals with forces provided by the French governor, and instructing the people whenever necessary.

Article 2: In each province there will be an *aga* of police, who will always remain with the French governor. He will have a guard of sixty armed men, with which he will move wherever necessary to maintain order and bring about obedience and tranquillity.

Article 3: In each province there will be a comptroller responsible for the collection of taxes and of the revenue formerly belonging to the Mamelukes, which today belong to the Republic; he will have the necessary agents under him. **(58)**

Cairo, 22 August 1798:

Article 1: An Egyptian Institute of Arts and Sciences will be established at Cairo.

Article 2: The principal objects will be: 1. The progress of knowledge and its propagation in Egypt. 2. Research, study and publication of the natural, industrial and historical facts about Egypt. 3. To give advice on the various questions upon which it may be consulted by the Government.

Article 3: The Institute will be divided into four sections of mathematics, physics, political economy and literature and the arts. Each section will consist of twelve members.

Article 7: There will be two sessions each decade, on Primidi and Sextidi. They will open at 7.0 a.m. and last for two hours.

Article 8: All general officers of the French army may attend all sessions. **(59)**

Cairo, 23 August 1798:

The Institute of Egypt assembled for the first time on 23 August 1798. Citizen Bonaparte proposed the following questions:

1. Can the ovens used to bake bread for the army be improved from the point of view of fuel consumption, and how?

2. Does there exist in Egypt anything to replace hops in the brewing of beer?

3. What are the customary methods of purifying and cooling the water of the Nile?

4. In the present circumstances in Cairo is it more suitable to construct wind or water mills?

5. Are there resources in Egypt for the manufacture of powder, and what are they?

6. What is the position in Egypt of law and education? What improvements in these matters are possible and desired by the people? **(60)**

The French installed in the house of Hassan Kyacheff a great library, with several librarians who kept guard over the books and handed them to those readers who needed them. This library was open daily from ten o'clock. The readers assembled in a large room next to the one where the books were kept. They sat down in chairs around large tables and started to work. Even simple privates went to work in the library. When a Moslem wished to visit the establishment he was not prevented from doing so, but on the contrary, was made very welcome. The French were particularly pleased when a Moslem visitor showed an interest in the sciences. I myself had occasion to visit that library. I saw, among other things, a large volume on the history of our Prophet (May God bless him!); his holy features were shown in it as the artists' knowledge permitted . . . I have seen many other books dealing with natural history, medicine, and applied mechanics. Some of the French were studying Arabic and learning verses from the Koran; in a word, they were great scholars and they loved the sciences, especially mathematics and philology. Day and night they applied themselves to Arabic . . . We were also shown a machine in which a glass was rotating; at the approach of a foreign body, the glass emitted sparks and produced a crackling sound. If a person held in his hand an object, even a mere wire, and touched the rotating glass with it, his body instantly received a shock that made the bones of his shoulders and arms crack. We were shown other experiments as well, all as extraordinary as the first one, such as intelligences like ours can neither conceive of nor explain. **(61)**

PROCEEDINGS OF THE INSTITUTE. *Cairo, 1 July 1799:*
A letter was read in which citizen Lancret, Member of the Institute reported that in the town of Rosetta citizen Bouchard, officer of Engineers, had discovered inscriptions the examination of which may afford a great deal of interest. On a black basalt stone these inscriptions were divided into three horizontal bands. The first from the bottom contains several lines in Greek characters, which were cut in the reign of Ptolemy Philopater; the second inscription is in unknown characters; and the third contains only hieroglyphics. **(62)**

What is known as the Rosetta Stone, now in the British Museum, was the most important of all the archaeological discoveries made by the French. Printed impressions were sent to scholars all over Europe but by the terms of the capitulation drawn up in 1801 the stone itself was surrendered to General Hutchinson, who sent it to London. There it was studied by many scholars, Dr Thomas Young being the first to use the Greek part to decipher some of the Egyptian hieroglyphics. In 1822 the French Egyptologist Champollion enlarged the vocabulary drawn up by Young and formulated a grammar which is the basis of our knowledge of ancient Egyptian writing.

The text enumerates the titles of Ptolemy V and the benefits conferred on Egypt by him, for which the priests decree various ceremonies to be observed in the temples. Dr Wallis Budge describes the triple inscription on the stone as follows:

The inscription on the Rosetta Stone is written in two languages, that is to say, in Egyptian and Greek. The Egyptian portion is cut upon it in: I. the Hieroglyphic character, that is to say in the old picture writing which was employed, from the earliest dynasties, for nearly all state and ceremonial documents that were intended to be seen by the public; and II. the Demotic character, that is to say the conventional, abbreviated and modified form of the Hieratic character, or cursive form of hieroglyphic writing, which was in use in the Ptolemaic period. The Greek portion of the inscription is cut in ordinary uncials . . .

The inscription is a copy of the Decree passed by the General Council of Egyptian priests assembled at Memphis to celebrate the first commemoration of the coronation of Ptolemy V, Epiphanes, king of all Egypt. The young king had been crowned in the eighth year of his reign, therefore the first commemoration took place in the ninth year, in the spring of the year B.C. 196.

The Mosque of El Azhar

This account of the Mosque of El Azhar shows how Bonaparte tried to win the support of the priests 'ulemas' (muftis) of Islam, but it is uncertain whether the incident described in the second part ever took place. The quotation is from Napoleon's MEMOIRS OF THE EGYPTIAN CAMPAIGN, which he dictated to his followers when in exile at St Helena. These memoirs (written in the third person according to the precedent set by Julius Caesar) aimed at inspiring a Napoleonic Legend, so that they are almost useless as historical evidence.

The school, or Sorbonne, of the Mosque El Azhar is the most celebrated in the East. It was founded by Saladin. There, sixty doctors or ulemas debated theology and explained the sacred texts. It was the only centre that could set an example and carry with it public opinion of the Islamic world . . . Napoleon neglected nothing to gain their favours and to flatter them. They were old men, worthy of respect for their morals, their erudition, their wealth, and even their birth. Every day at sunrise they would come to his palace before prayer time. They came on their richly harnessed mules, surrounded by their servants and by many runners armed with poles. The French sentries presented arms to them. In the palace they were received with respect; sherberts and coffee were served to them. After a moment the General would enter, sit down in their midst, on the same divan, and seek to gain their trust by discussing the Koran, and by displaying great admiration for the Prophet. When they left, they went to the mosques, where the people were assembled. There they spoke to them of their hopes and calmed the distrust and hostility of that immense population. They rendered great services to the army . . .

When he thought the right moment had arrived, he said to ten of the principal sheiks, those who were most devoted to him, 'We must put an end to these disorders. I need a *fetfa* (proclamation) of the Mosque of El Azhar, ordering the people to make an oath of obedience.' This request made them turn pale. Their faces showed the fright in their souls. They became sullen and embarrassed. The sheik El Charkawi, head of the ulemas of El Azhar, asked to be heard and said, 'You want the protection of the Prophet, who loves you. You want the Moslem Arabs to enlist under your flag. You want to restore the glory of Arabia, and you are not an idolater. Then become a Moslem yourself. A hundred thousand Egyptians, a hundred thousand Arabs will come to join you from Arabia, from Mecca and Medina. With them under your leadership and discipline, you will conquer the East and you will restore the Prophet's fatherland in all its glory'. When he said this, the old men's faces became wreathed in smiles. All prostrated themselves to implore divine protection. It was the General's turn to be astonished. **(63)**

Uprising and Plague

Nicholas, a Turkish chronicler, describes how the behaviour of the French led to an uprising on 21 October. It was suppressed after a bombardment of the Mosque of El Azhar. Describing the reprisals to General

Reynier, Bonaparte said, 'Every night we have about thirty heads chopped off, many of them belonging to the ringleaders. This I believe will teach them a good lesson'.

The presence of the French in Cairo was intolerable, especially when Egyptians saw their wives and daughters walking in the streets unveiled and appearing to be the property of the French, with whom they were seen in public and with whom they cohabited. Before these facts, the Moslems died of shame. It was bad enough for them to see the taverns that had been established in bazaars of Cairo and even in several mosques. Such a spectacle created an intolerable atmosphere for the Moslems. Fundamentally, the French occupation improved the condition of the lower classes—the second-hand dealers, pack carriers, artisans, donkey drivers, horse grooms, pimps and prostitutes. All told, the scum of the populace was doing well, because it benefited from the new freedom. But the élite and the middle classes experienced all sorts of vexations, because imports and exports had come to a standstill. **(64)**

Bonaparte continued to write optimistic letters to the Directory, such as this; but the bloody repression of the Cairo revolt meant that his rule was insecure, and his anxiety about the spread of bubonic plague was one of the reasons why he embarked on the Syrian campaign. BONAPARTE TO THE DIRECTORY *from HQ Cairo, 17 December 1798:*

I am sending you an officer from the Army with orders to stay only seven or eight days in Paris and then to return to Cairo. Egypt begins to be organised. A boat arrived at Suez which brought an Indian, who had a letter for the commander of the French forces in Egypt; but this letter has been lost. It seems that our arrival in Egypt has given a great impression of our power in India and produced effects very unfavourable to the British. There is fighting there.

We are still without news from France; not a single courier since Messidor. That is unparalleled even in the colonies. My brother (Jerome) Quartermaster Sucy and several couriers I have sent to you should have arrived. Send ships for us to Damietta.

The English (under Sir Sidney Smith) have three battleships and two frigates before Alexandria. General Desaix is in Upper Egypt chasing Murad Bey, who is fleeing before him with a force of Mamelukes. General Bon is at Suez.

Work is proceeding with the greatest activity on the fortifications of Alexandria, Rosetta, Damietta, Bilbeis, Salhiya, Suez and Cairo. The army is in the best possible condition and has few sick. There are concentrations of Turkish forces in Syria; I would have had an argument with them if seven days of desert did not separate us. We have goods in abundance, but money is very scarce and the presence of the English ships stops all trade.

We await news of France and Europe: that is a great need for our spirits. **(65)**

BONAPARTE TO GENERAL MARMONT, *Governor of Alexandria, from HQ Cairo, 28 January 1799:*
I cannot understand the obstinacy of Commissary Michaix in staying in his house when there is plague there; why does he not go and camp on a hillock near Pompey's column?

Keep all your battalions at least half a league apart. Keep very few troops in the city and, since it is the most dangerous spot, no corps d'élite. As for the unfortunate light infantry demi-brigade, have them strip and take a good sea bath, scrubbing themselves from head to foot; have them wash their clothes well, and see to it that they keep themselves clean. Have no parades and mount no guards except in each camp. Have a big ditch dug and filled with quick-lime to throw the dead into. Order everyone to wash face, hands and feet daily and to keep clean.

If you cannot save the whole of the units, where this disease has broken out, at least save the majority of your garrison. It seems to me that you have not yet taken steps commensurate with the circumstances. If I did not have stores in Alexandria that I cannot do without, I would already have told you to take your garrison and camp three leagues away in the desert. I know you cannot do that, but approach as near to it as possible. **(66)**

CHAPTER FOUR

THE SYRIAN CAMPAIGN (1799)

The Ottoman Empire having declared war on the French, Bonaparte was compelled to march north into Syria in order to anticipate an invasion of Egypt. At that date the Pashalik of Syria comprised the modern Israel, Jordan, Lebanon and Syria. Its governor was Achmet Pasha, known as Djezzar, 'the Butcher'. He was a fierce old man of Bosnian birth, who had been a Mameluke slave before being appointed to this important post. He lived at St Jean d'Acre, where the crusader castle of Richard Coeur de Lion still stood, though in a dilapidated condition.

Neither Djezzar's small fortress, nor his unreliable garrison could have withstood Bonaparte's army had it not been for the presence of two British warships, the *Tigre* and *Theseus*, under the command of Sir Sidney Smith, who had with him a French emigré friend, Le Picard de Phélipeaux, an engineer of genius. They were two very remarkable men. Smith was the embodiment of the romantic adventurer, though his egotism and theatrical temperament did not make him popular in the service. Early in the war he landed in France to promote a Royalist insurrection, but was captured and confined to the Temple prison, from which he escaped with the assistance of Phélipeaux. The latter had been in the same class as Bonaparte at the military academy, where the two men seem to have disliked each other from the start. Phélipeaux graduated with first-class honours, his Corsican rival's academic career being much less distinguished. Both began their careers as lieutenants in the artillery.

Soon after the Battle of the Nile, Smith was sent to the Levant with special powers to negotiate with the Porte, to which his brother Spencer Smith was attached as a diplomatist. He arrogated to himself the title of Commodore (much to the annoyance of Nelson, his superior officer), as well as the functions of ambassador (equally to the annoyance of Lord Elgin, who arrived in that capacity after the campaign was over). In March 1799 he took over the command of the small squadron cruising off Alexandria, moving north to Acre just in time to defend the town in the heroic fashion described in these documents. This check to Bonaparte's career, besides illustrating the flexible nature of sea power, caused the lasting hatred which the latter conceived for Smith. As he admitted at St Helena, 'If it had not been for the English, I should have been Emperor of the East, but wherever there is water to float a ship, we are sure to find you in our way . . . I should have reached Constantinople and India. I should have changed the face of the world.'

His object at the beginning of 1799 was to defeat Djezzar Pasha. Leaving Cairo on 10 February, he occupied El Arish, the frontier town, after the hardships of a march across the desert of Sinai. Thence he continued to Gaza and Jaffa, which had to be taken by storm. Here a massacre of Turkish prisoners left a stain on his reputation, and the outbreak of plague gave a foretaste of dangers to come. On 17 March from his headquarters on Mount Carmel, he saw to his surprise Smith's warships lying off Acre. The French siege artillery was proceeding by sea. Bonaparte's efforts to stop it before it fell into the hands of Smith proved unavailing, so that by the time the siege commenced Djezzar's defences had been strengthened with guns and seamen. Even these would have proved ineffective against the repeated French assaults had not Turkish reinforcements arrived by sea. Elsewhere, hostile forces attacking the French in the Damascus area were defeated at the Battle of Mount Tabor. Wherever French troops under Bonaparte or Kléber met the Turks in open battle, they defeated them.

The stubborn defence of Acre was another matter. The loss of his finest troops in fruitless attacks, together with the incidence of plague, compelled Bonaparte to raise the siege on 20 May. The retreat along the coast road reminds one of the more famous retreat from Moscow; the route had been devastated during the advance, the heat was intolerable and disease was rife. Yet on 14 June the remnants of the army entered Cairo as if it was victorious.

On 15 July a seaborne invasion of Egypt by a Turkish army was made at Aboukir Bay. Within a fortnight Bonaparte had concentrated enough troops to rout it on the peninsula, from which there was no escape but by swimming to the ships. It is a curious fact that one who escaped in this way was an Albanian named Mehemet Ali, later to become the father of modern Egypt.

Smith was only a spectator of the catastrophe, but he took care that newspapers should reach Bonaparte informing him of what was going on in Europe—the Austrian invasion of Italy; the Russian entry into the Adriatic; the failure of the Brest fleet intended for his relief to get further than Toulon; the internecine plots of the Directory, which proved that the Republic was on the verge of anarchy. Talleyrand, so largely responsible for the Egyptian expedition, had resigned. Lucien Bonaparte was president of the Council of Five Hundred. Everything conspired to convince him that he must get back to France.

Without warning Kléber that he was to be left in command of the army, on the night of 22 August Bonaparte sailed from Alexandria with a select band of generals, as well as his Mameluke servant Roustan, who became his bodyguard for the next ten years. Though sighted by Keith's frigates off the Riviera, Bonaparte's luck held because the *Muiron* and *Carrère* were thought to be British ships. He landed at Fréjus on 9 October and a month later carried out the coup d'état of the 18th Brumaire. The Directory was over. The Consulate had begun. But the best army France possessed remained isolated in Egypt.

The Syrian Threat

From Napoleon's account of the reasons for the Syrian campaign in his MEMOIRS, *composed when in exile at St Helena:*

Two Turkish armies assembled, one at Rhodes, and the other in Syria to attack the French in Egypt. It appears that they were to act simultaneously in the month of May, the first landing at Aboukir, and the second by crossing the desert which divides Syria from Egypt. At the beginning of January news arrived that Djezzar Pasha had been appointed commander of the army in Syria; that his vanguard, under the command of Abdullah, had already arrived at El Arish, had occupied that place and was engaged in repairing the fort, which may be considered as the key of Egypt on the Syrian side. A train of artillery of forty guns, served by 1,200 cannoneers, the only troops of that empire that had been trained in the European manner, had landed at Jaffa; considerable magazines were forming in that town; and a great number of transports, part of which came from Constantinople. At Gaza stores of skins to hold water had been formed; report said that there were enough of them to enable an army of 60,000 men to cross the desert.

If the French had remained quiet in Egypt, they would certainly have been attacked by the two armies at once; it was also to be feared that the Turks would be joined by a body of European troops, and that the attack would be made at the moment of internal troubles. The rules of war, therefore, required me to anticipate my enemies, to cross the great desert during the winter, to possess myself of all the magazines which the enemy had formed on the coast of Syria, and to attack and destroy the troops in succession as fast as they collected . . .

We might, if fortunate, have been on the Euphrates by the middle of the summer, with 100,000 auxiliaries, who would have had a reserve of 25,000 French veterans, some of the best troops in the world, with a numerous train of artillery. Constantinople would then have been menaced; and if an amicable arrangement could have been formed with the Porte, we might have crossed the desert and marched on the Indus by the end of the autumn. (67)

BONAPARTE TO DIRECTORY *from HQ Cairo, 10 February 1799:*
Citizen Directors . . . The English have persuaded the Porte that Djezzar Pasha, in addition to his own pashalic of Acre, should have that of Damascus. Ibrahim, Abdullah and other pasha are at Gaza and threatening to invade Egypt. I am leaving at once to find them. That means nine days of desert with neither grass nor water, but I have collected a considerable number of camels and hope that we shall lack nothing. When you read this letter, it is possible that I shall be on the ruins of Solomon's city.

Djezzar Pasha is a fierce old man of seventy with an unreasoning hatred of the French. He has replied with scorn to the friendly overtures I have several times made to him. I have three aims in the operation I am undertaking.

1. To assure the conquest of Egypt by the establishment of a strong point beyond the desert which will hold armies, of whatever nation, so far from Egypt that they cannot combine with an European army landing on the coast.

2. To force the Porte to take up a position, thereby supporting the negotiations which you have no doubt begun.

3. To prevent the English cruisers from drawing supplies from Syria by using the two months of winter left to me in making the whole of that coast friendly through war and negotiation. (68)

Three copies of these INSTRUCTIONS, *dated 4 November 1798 were sent, signed by the Directory, although the real author was Talleyrand. Only one reached Bonaparte on 25 March 1799, by which time he was besieging Acre.*
You must, at least for some time to come, manage to shift for yourself. In this respect, everything you have done to attach the native population to your

21 *An officer of the French Imperial Guard by Géricault*

cause deserves our approval. Since we cannot send you any help, the Executive Directory knows better than to give you any orders or even instructions. You will determine your line of conduct according to your own position and to the means you dispose of in Egypt . . . Since it would be difficult, at the present moment, to make possible your return to France, there are three choices open to you: either to remain in Egypt and to establish yourself in such a manner as to be safe from a Turkish attack (but you are aware that for part of the year the country is extremely unhealthy for Europeans, especially if you receive no assistance from the homeland); or to march to India, where, if you get there, you will no doubt find men ready to join you to fight the English domination; or finally, to march on Constantinople and to meet the enemy who is threatening you. The choice is up to you and to the brave and distinguished men who surround you. **(69)**

The march through Palestine to Acre in Syria is described by Captain Vertray.

The following day (February 6) General Kléber's division rejoined us. The General had recovered from the wound he had received at Alexandria. As he was beloved and esteemed by all, our division gave him a warm welcome. We had often admired his bravery and his martial bearing, and his return to the head of his troops was a regular fête for the camp. Kléber was the soldier's friend in the fullest meaning of the term, for if he was strict during actions or parades, in the camp he was most careful of the well-being and happiness of his men. From all sides our soldiers ran before him and saluted him; during the evening he walked in the camp, his tall figure and erect carriage, his just and courageous appearance inspiring respect and sympathy.

On February 16 and 17 the army rested and order was given to issue rations for four days and make provision for water; in fact, we should meet neither spring nor pool before El Arish. The soldiers were warned that they would not find a drop of water en route, and everyone had to make the best arrangements he could to alleviate the sufferings of this difficult march . . .

For my part, in common with other officers, I did not think St Jean d'Acre would offer any serious resistance. We were, in fact, too much accustomed to reckon on the inferiority of our enemies. In the evening the siege work began, without waiting for the pieces of heavy cannon which were being sent from Alexandria (and were captured by the English). Three 12-pounders only were put into a battery and opened fire on the part of the town which faced our camp. The rampart opposite the army presented a salient angle, at the apex of which was a tower, the fire from which caused great losses to our troops. The tower was defended on its left by the two English ships, *Theseus* and *Tigre*, under the command of Sir Sidney Smith.

On 27 March my battalion had to repel a sortie by the enemy, which it did without much loss. It was the following day that the first assault was attempted . . . The check of this assault gave the besieged confidence. Sidney Smith gave the direction of the defence to a French emigré, a retired Engineer officer named Phélipeaux. The Turkish batteries were served by English gunners. The almost daily sorties of the garrison caused us great losses. On our side ammunition ran short; the army was fatigued by the constant labours and painful duties; provisions became scarce, the whole country being devastated and deserted. **(70)**

The French at Jaffa

BONAPARTE TO DJEZZAR PASHA *from HQ Jaffa, 9 March 1799:*

Since my entry into Egypt I have several times informed you that it was not my intention to make war on you and that my sole aim was to destroy the Mamelukes; you have not replied to any of the overtures I have made. I have let you know that I wished you to remove Ibrahim Bey from the frontier of Egypt: far from that, you have sent troops to Gaza, you have set up great stores, you have spread it abroad that you were going to enter Egypt and you have effected your invasion by putting 2,000 of your troops into the fort of El Arish, which is ten leagues inside the territory of Egypt. I have therefore had to leave Cairo and bring to you the war that you seemed to be provoking.

The provinces of Gaza, Ramleh and Jaffa are in my power . . . In a few days I shall march on Acre. But what reason should I have for shortening by a few years the life of an old man whom I do not know? What are a few more leagues beside the country I have already conquered? And, since God gives me victory, I wish, like him, to be merciful, not only towards the people but also towards the great.

You have no real reason to be my enemy, since you were the enemy of the Mamelukes. Your pashalic is separated from Egypt by the provinces of Gaza and Ramleh and by immense deserts. Become my friend again and enemy of the Mamelukes and the English: I will do you as much good as I can otherwise do you harm. Send me your answer by a man entrusted with full powers who knows your intentions; he will present himself at my outposts with a white flag, and I am ordering my staff to send you a safe conduct, which you will find here attached.

On the 24th of this month I shall be on the march for Acre; I must, therefore, have your reply before that day. (71)

After Jaffa was stormed on 7 March over 3,000 prisoners were massacred, partly because Bonaparte had no means of feeding them, partly to impress Djezzar Pasha at Acre. The writer was an assistant paymaster in the Army.
CITIZEN PEYROUSSE TO HIS MOTHER AT CARCASSONNE:
That, in a city taken by storm, the infuriated troops should loot, burn and kill whatever comes their way, is something demanded by the laws of war, and humanity covers these horrors with a veil. But that two or three days after the attack, when passions have calmed down, one should order in cold blooded savagery the murder of 3,000 men who have surrendered to us in good faith! Posterity will no doubt pass judgement on this atrocity, and those who ordered it will find their place among the butchers of humanity.

About 3,000 men put down their arms and were instantly led to our camp. By order of the commander-in-chief, the Egyptians, Moroccans and Turks were separated. The next morning, all the Moroccans, were taken to the sea shore and two battalions began to shoot them down. Their only hope of saving their lives was to throw themselves into the sea; they did not hesitate, and all tried to escape by swimming. They were shot at leisure, and in an instant the sea was red with blood and covered with corpses. A few were lucky enough to reach some rocks. Soldiers were ordered to follow them in boats and finish them off.

Once this execution was over, we fondly hoped that it would not be repeated and that the other prisoners would be spared. Our hopes were soon disappointed, when the next day, 1,200 Turkish artillerymen, who for two days had been kept without food in front of General Bonaparte's tent, were taken to be executed. The soldiers had been carefully instructed not to waste their ammunition, and they were ferocious enough to stab them with their bayonets. Among the victims, we found many children, who in the act of death clung to their fathers. This example will teach our enemies that they cannot count on French good faith, and sooner or later the blood of these 3,000 victims will be upon us. (72)

At the same time as the massacre, there was a serious outbreak of bubonic plague in the army. The following scene from the MEMOIRS OF DR DESGENETTES, *the senior physician, inspired the picture by Baron Gros which became famous among Napoleon's followers. However, on his return to Jaffa after his defeat at Acre, those who still survived were deliberately poisoned with opium because they could not join the retreat. Desgenettes himself refused to carry out the order.*

On March 11, 1799, General Bonaparte, followed by his general staff, felt that he himself should visit the hospital. He walked through the hospital and its annex, spoke to almost all the soldiers who were conscious enough to hear him, and for an hour and a half, with the greatest calm, busied himself with the details of the administration. While in a very small and crowded ward, he helped to lift, or rather carry, the hideous corpse of a soldier whose torn uniform was soiled by the spontaneous bursting of an enormous bubo. After several attempts to lead the General back to the door, I was forced to tell him positively that a longer stay would be worse than useless. (73)

The Defence of Acre

These two DESPATCHES *by Captain Sir Sidney Smith to Admiral St Vincent, Commander-in-Chief in the Mediterranean, describe his organisation of the defence of Acre and his capture of the French siege train. During the siege his friend Phélipeaux died of fever.* Tigre *off St Jean d'Acre, 23 March 1799:*

My Lord, I have the honour to inform you that in consequence of intelligence from Djezzar Pasha, Governor of Syria, of the incursions of General Bonaparte's army into that province and his approach to its capital at Acre, I hastened with a portion of the naval force to arrive there two days before the enemy made his appearance.

Much was done in this interval under the direction of Captain Miller of the *Theseus* and Colonel Phélipeaux towards putting the place in a better state of

22 *Bonaparte visiting victims of the bubonic plague at Jaffa by Gros*

defence to resist the attacks of European army, and the presence of a British naval force appeared to encourage and decide the Pasha and his troops to make a vigorous resistance.

The enemy's advance guard was discovered at the foot of Mount Carmel on the night of the 17th by the *Tigre's* guard boats; these troops, not expecting to find a naval force of any description in Syria, took up their ground close to the waterside and were consequently exposed to the fire of grape shot from the boats, which put them to rout the instant it opened upon them and obliged them to retreat precipitately up the side of the Mount. The main body of the enemy, finding the road between Mount Carmel and the sea thus exposed, came in by that of Nazareth, and invested the town of Acre to the east, but not without being much harassed by the Samaritan Arabs, who are even more inimical to the French than the Egyptians. As the enemy returned our fire by musketry only, it was evident that they had not brought cannon with them, which were therefore to be expected by sea, and measures were taken accordingly for intercepting them. The *Theseus* being already detached off Jaffa, the enemy's flotilla, which came in from the sea, fell in with and captured the *Torride*, and was coming round Mount Carmel when it was discovered from the *Tigre* as consisting of a corvette and nine sail of gun vessels; on seeing us, they hauled off. The alacrity of the ship's company in making sail after them was highly praiseworthy; our guns soon reached them and seven struck. The corvette containing Bonaparte's private property and two small vessels escaped, since it became an object to secure the prizes without chasing further, their cargoes consisting the battering train of artillery, ammunition etc., destined for the siege of Acre, being much wanted for its defence. The prizes were accordingly anchored off the town, manned from the ships, and immediately employed in harassing the enemy's posts, impeding his approaches and covering

the ship's boats sent further in shore to cut off his supplies. These have been constantly occupied in these services for these five days and nights past, and such has been the zeal of their crews that they have requested not to be relieved after many hours excessive labour at the guns and oars. **(74)**

Tigre, *7 April 1799:*

. . . Captain Wilmot had been so indefatigable in mounting the prize-guns under the direction of an able officer of the Engineers, Colonel Phélipeaux, that the fire therefrom had already slackened that of the enemy; still, however, much was to be apprehended from the effects of the mine, and a sortie was determined on, in which the British marines and seamen were to force their way into it, while the Turkish troops attacked the enemy's trenches on the right and left.

The sally took place this morning just before daylight. The impetuosity and noise of the Turks rendered the attempt to surprise the enemy abortive, though in other respects they did their part well. Lieutenant Wright, who commanded the seamen pioneers, notwithstanding he received two shots in his right arm as he advanced, entered the mine with the pikemen, and proceeded to the bottom of it, where he verified its direction and destroyed all that could be destroyed in its then state by pulling down its supporters. Colonel Douglas supported the seamen in this desperate service with his usual gallantry under the increased fire of the enemy, bringing off Lt. Wright, who had scarcely strength left to get out of the enemy's trench . . .

The result of our day's work is that we have taught the besiegers to respect the enemy they have to deal with, so as to keep at a greater distance. The apprehension of the garrison are quieted as to the effects of the mine, which we have besides learned to countermine, and more time is gained for the arrival

23 *Sir Sidney Smith from the portrait by Eckstein*

of the reinforcements daily expected. **(75)**

Bonaparte had sent Citizen Beauchamp to Constanti-
nople to negotiate. On his way he was captured by
Smith, who took this opportunity on 8 May 1799 of
calling on Bonaparte to surrender. He received no
reply, because by this time Bonaparte had conceived a
personal hatred for him which lasted all his life. At St
Helena he often told a story that Smith sent him a
challenge to a duel, which he refused, saying he would
not have accepted it from the great Marlborough
himself. Smith denies that such a challenge was ever
sent.

Monsieur le Général, Since your instructions to your
emissary Beauchamp contain these words: 'If you
are asked whether the French would agree to leave
Egypt', along with your reply 'Why not?' I believe
I may send you the enclosed proclamation of the
Ottoman Porte without your finding it out of place.
I did not want to ask you the question 'Are the French
willing to leave Syria?' before you had a chance to
match your strength against ours, since you could
not be persuaded, as I am, of the impracticability of
your enterprise. But now that you can see that Acre
becomes stronger each day instead of being weakened
by two months of siege, I do ask you this: 'Are you
willing to evacuate your troops from the territory of
the Ottoman Empire before the intervention of the
great allied army changes the nature of this question?'

You may believe me, Monsieur le Général, that
my only motive in asking you this is my desire to
avoid further bloodshed. I have the honour, etc.

SIDNEY SMITH. (76)

In another DESPATCH TO ST VINCENT, *Smith describes*
the repulse of the main attack on the citadel at Acre.
Tigre, *Acre, 9 May 1799:*

I had the honour to inform your Lordship that we
were employed completing two ravelins [outworks]
for the reception of cannon to flank the enemy's

nearest approaches, distant only ten yards from them. They were attacked that very night, and almost every night since, but the enemy have each time been repulsed with heavy loss. They have continued to batter in the breach with progressive success, and have nine several times attempted to storm, but have as often been beat back with immense slaughter. Our best mode of defence has been frequent sorties to keep them on the defence and impede the progress of their covering works. We have thus been in one continual battle ever since the beginning of the siege, interrupted only at short intervals by the excessive fatigue of every individual on both sides.

We have long been anxiously looking for a reinforcement, without which we could not expect to be able to keep the place so long as we have. The delay in its arrival being occasioned by Hassan Bey's having originally received orders to join me in Egypt; I was obliged to be very preremptory in the repetition of my orders for him to join me here; it was not, however, till the evening of the day before yesterday, the fifty-first of the siege, that his fleet of corvettes and transports made its appearance. The approach of this additional strength was the signal to Bonaparte for a most vigorous and persevering assault in hopes to get possession of the town before the reinforcements to the garrison could disembark . . .

The fire of the besieged was much slackened in comparison to that of the besiegers, and our flanking fire was become of less effect, the enemy having covered themselves in this lodgement by two traverses across the ditch, which they had constructed under the fire that had been opposed to them the whole night, and which were now composed of sand bags and the bodies of their dead, built in with them, their bayonets alone being visible above them.

Hassan Bey's troops were in the boats, though as yet but half way on shore; this was the most critical point of the contest and an effort was necessary to preserve the place for a short time till their arrival. I accordingly landed the boats at the mole and took the crews up to the breach armed with pikes. The enthusiastic gratitude of the Turks, men, women and children, at the sight of such a reinforcement at such a time is not to be described; many fugitives returned with us to the breach, which we found defended by a few brave Turks, whose destructive weapons were heavy stones which, striking the assailants on the head, overthrew the foremost down the slope and impeded the progress of the rest.

Djezzar Pasha, hearing that the English were on the breach, quitted his station where, according to ancient Turkish custom, he was sitting to reward such as should bring him the heads of the enemy, and distributing musket cartridges with his own hands. The energetic old man, coming behind us, pulled us down with violence, saying if any harm happened to his English friends all was lost. This amicable contest as to who should defend the breach occasioned a rush of Turks to the spot, and thus time was gained for the arrival of Hassan Bey's troops.

The groups of generals and aide-de-camps, which the shells of the 68-pounders had frequently dispersed, were now reassembled on Richard Coeur de Lion's mount. Bonaparte was distinguishable in the centre of the semi-circle; his gesticulation indicated a renewal of attack, and his despatching an aide-de-camp to the camp showed that he waited only for a reinforcement. I gave directions for Hassan Bey's ships to take station in the shoal water to the southward and made the *Tigre's* signal to weigh and join the *Theseus* to the northward.

A little before sunset a massive column appeared, advancing to the breach with solemn step. The Pasha's idea was not to defend the breach at this time, but rather to let a certain number of the enemy in, and then close with them, according to the Turkish mode of war. The column thus mounted the breach unmolested and descended from the rampart into the Pasha's garden, where, in a very few minutes, the bravest and most advanced among them lay headless corpses, the sabre, with the addition of a dagger in the other hand, proving more than a match for the bayonet; the rest retreated precipitately and the commanding officer, who was seen manfully encouraging his men to mount the breach, and whom we have since learned to be General Lannes, was carried off wounded by a musket shot . . .

Bonaparte will, no doubt, renew the attack, the breach being as above described, perfectly practicable for fifty men abreast; indeed, the town is not, nor ever has been, defensible according to the rules of art; but according to every other rule, it must and shall be defended; not that by itself it is worth defending, but we feel that it is by this breach Bonaparte means to march to further conquests. 'Tis on the issue of this conflict that depends the opinion of the multitude of spectators on the surrounding hills, who wait only to see how it ends to join the victors; and with such a reinforcement for the execution of his known projects, Constantinople and even Vienna must feel the shock.

Be assured, my lord, the magnitude of our obligations does but increase the energy of our efforts in the attempt to discharge our duty; and though we may, and probably shall be overpowered, I can venture to say that the French army will be so much further weakened, before it prevails, as to be little able to profit by its dear bought victory. (77)

Retreat to Egypt

BONAPARTE'S DESPATCH, *written the day after the assault had failed, hints at the prospect of a retreat to Egypt. HQ before Acre, 10 May 1799:*
Citizen Directors, You have seen from my last despatch the speed with which the army crossed the desert, the capture of El Arish, Gaza, Jaffa, and the dispersal of the enemy army, which had lost its magazines and part of its camels, waterskins and field equipment. There were still two months before the

right season for landings; I resolved to pursue the remnants of the enemy army and to maintain the war for two months in the heart of Syria. We marched on Acre . . .

Today we occupy the principal points of the rampart. The enemy has built a second defence line based on Djezzar's castle. It would remain for us to advance into the town. That would mean besieging every house and losing more men than I wish to. Besides, it is too late in the season; what I intended has been done; Egypt calls me.

I am going to set up a battery of 24-pounders to destroy Djezzar's palace and the principal buildings of the town. I shall send in 1,000 bombs and that should do a lot of damage in so restricted a space. When I have reduced Acre to a heap of rubble, I shall recross the desert and be ready to receive a European or Turkish army, which will land in Egypt in Messidor or Thermidor . . .

I have been completely satisfied with the army in all events and in a type of warfare so new to Europeans. It has shown that true courage and warlike talents are surprised at nothing and accept privations of every kind. The result, we hope, will be an advantageous peace and an accession of glory and prosperity for the Republic. (78)
Almost every detail in the following PROCLAMATION *was untrue, and the soldiers must have known it; but Bonaparte issued it for the benefit of posterity. HQ before Acre, 17 May 1799:*
Soldiers, you have crossed the desert dividing Africa from Asia faster than an Arab army.

The army that was marching to invade Egypt has been destroyed; you have captured its general, its field equipment, its waterskins, its camels. You have taken all the forts defending the desert wells.

On the field of Mount Tabor you dispersed that horde of men who had run from every corner of Asia in the hopes of looting Egypt.

The thirty ships you saw arrive before Acre twelve

days ago carried the army which was intended to besiege Alexandria; but it was forced to come to the help of Acre and there met its fate. Some of its flags will decorate your entry into Egypt.

Thus, having made war in the heart of Syria for three months, having taken forty field guns, fifty flags and 6,000 prisoners, having razed to the ground the fortifications of Gaza, Jaffa, Haifa, Acre, and all with a handful of men, we are going back to Egypt. The season for landings calls me there.

In a few days you might have hoped to capture the Pasha himself in his palace; but at this time of year the capture of the castle of Acre is not worth the loss of a few days, and besides, the brave men I should lose there are now needed for more essential operations.

Soldiers, we have a hard and dangerous road to cross; we have stopped the East from doing anything against us this campaign, but we may have to repel efforts from the West.

That will give you new opportunities for glory; and if in the midst of so many struggles each day brings the death of a brave man, new men must step forward to take their place in the front rank among those few who take the lead in danger and command victory. (79)

In his final DESPATCH TO THE DIRECTORY *Bonaparte explains why he has begun the retreat to Egypt. HQ Jaffa, 27 May 1799:*

I informed you, Citizen Directors, in my despatch of 21 Floréal [10 May] of the glorious events of the last three months in Syria and of my resolution to recross the desert quickly and return to Egypt before June.

As I said, the batteries of mortars and 24-pounders were set up during 23 Floréal to destroy the palace of Djezzar and the principal buildings of Acre; they fired for twenty-four hours and produced the effect I intended. The town was on fire throughout.

25 *The Battle of Mount Tabor by Cogniet*

On 27 Floréal the desperate garrison made a general sortie. The fight lasted three hours; General Verdier was commanding the trench. The rest of the troops, which arrived from Constantinople on the 19th and were European-trained, fell upon our trenches in close column. We withdrew the posts we were holding on the ramparts, and thereby our field batteries were able to pour case shot on them at 150 yards. Nearly half of them fell on the field.

It seemed a favourable moment to carry the town. But deserters and prisoners and our spies all agreed in their reports that the plague was raging horribly in Acre, more than sixty people dying daily, and that the symptoms were terrible and within thirty-six hours caused the victims to fall into convulsions like those of rabies. It would have been impossible to prevent the soldiers from looting once they were scattered in the town, and at night they would have brought into the camp the germs of that terrible scourge, more to be feared than all the armies in the world. The army left Acre on 2 Praireal and reached Tantura that evening. My next despatch will be dated from Cairo. **(80)**

Writing to Nelson, his superior officer, Smith gives a jubilant account of the proceedings at Acre, from Tigre, *off Acre, 30 May 1799:*

My Lord, The Providence of Almighty God has been wonderfully manifested in the defeat and precipitate retreat of the French army, the means we had of opposing its gigantic efforts against us being totally inadequate of themselves to the production of such a result. The measure of their iniquities seems to have been filled by the massacre of Turkish prisoners at Jaffa in cold blood three days after their capture, and the plain of Nazareth has been the boundary of Bonaparte's extraordinary career.

He raised the siege of Acre on May 20, leaving

26 *While Bonaparte was in Syria, the Turks attacked at Aboukir on 15 July 1799* all his heavy artillery behind him, either buried or thrown into the sea, where, however, it was easily visible and can be weighed . . .

General Kléber's division had been sent eastward towards the fords of the Jordan to oppose the Damascus army. It was recalled from hence to take its turn in the daily efforts to mount the breach at Acre, in which every other division in succession had failed, with the loss of their bravest men and three-quarters of their officers. It seems much was hoped from this division as it had, by its firmness and the steady front it opposed in the form of a hollow square, kept upwards of 10,000 men in check during a whole day in the plain between Nazareth and Mount Tabor, till Bonaparte came with his horse artillery and extricated these troops, dispersing the multitude of irregular cavalry by which they were completely surrounded . . .

The utmost disorder has been manifested in the retreat and the whole track between Acre and Gaza is strewed with the dead bodies of those who have sunk under fatigue or the effects of slight wounds; such as could walk, unfortunately for them, not having been embarked. The rowing gunboats annoyed the van column of the retreating army in its march along the beach and the Arabs harassed its rear when it turned inland to avoid their fire. We observed the smoke of musketry behind the sandhills from the attack of a party of them which came down to our boats and touched our flag with every token of union and respect. The Governor of Jerusalem, to whom notice was sent of Bonaparte's retreat, having entered Jaffa by land at the same time that we brought our guns to bear on it by sea, a stop was put to the massacre and pillage already begun by the Nablusians. The English flag, rehoisted in the consul's house, under which the Pasha met me, serves as an asylum for all religions and every description of the surviving inhabitants. The heaps of unburied Frenchmen, lying on the bodies of those whom they massacred two months ago, afford another proof of divine justice, which has caused these murderers to perish by the infection arising from their own atrocious act. Seven poor wretches are left alive in the hospital; they are protected and shall be taken care of.

Note by Sir Sidney Smith from Nazareth.
I am just returned from the Cave of the Annunciation, where secretly and alone I have been returning thanks to the Almighty for our late wonderful success. Well may we exclaim 'the race is not always to the swift, nor the battle to the strong'. **(81)**

Bonaparte embarks for France

Bonaparte left Cairo for France on 18 August. Waiting to embark at Alexandria on board two frigates under Admiral Ganteaume, he gave these INSTRUCTIONS TO GENERAL MENOU *to hand to Kléber, who had received no warning of his departure for France. The naval squadron mentioned never reached Egypt. HQ Alexandria, 22 August 1799:*
You will find enclosed, Citizen General, an order to assume command of the army. Fear that the English squadron may re-appear at any moment causes me to hasten my departure by two or three days.

I am taking with me Generals Berthier, Lannes, Murat, Andréossy and Marmont, and citizens Monge and Berthollet.

Enclosed are English and Frankfurt newspapers up to 10 June. You will see from them that we have lost Italy; that Mantua, Turin and Tortona are besieged. I have reason to hope that the first of these fortresses will hold out till the end of November. If fortune smiles on me, I expect to reach Europe by the beginning of October. You will find attached a cipher for correspondence with the Government and another for correspondence with me.

27 *'The Deserter of the Army of Egypt' by Gillray*

92

BUONAPARTÉ leaving EGYPT.

For an illustration of the above, see the Intercepted Letters from the Republican General Kleber, to the French Directory,
respecting the Courage, Honor, & Patriotic Views, of "the Deserter of the Army of Egypt."

During October, please send off Junot and the belongings which I have left at Cairo and my servants. But I shall not mind if you take any you wish into your own service.

The Government wishes General Desaix to leave for Europe during November, unless serious events occur.

The Commission of the Arts will return to France in November as soon as they have completed their mission, under a safe conduct that you must request under the exchange agreement. At the moment they are finishing their work in visiting Upper Egypt. But you will have no difficulty in retaining any you think may be useful.

The arrival of our Brest Squadron at Toulon and of the Spanish squadron at Cartagena leaves no doubt as to the possibility of transporting to Egypt the muskets, sabres, pistols and shot which you need and of which I have an exact list, together with enough recruits to make good the losses of two campaigns. The Government will then itself let you know its intentions, and I myself, both as public man and as a private individual, will take steps to send you frequent news.

Should unforeseen events render all our efforts fruitless, and you have not received help or news from France by May and if, despite all precautions, there is plague in Egypt this year which kills off 1,500 of your men, a serious loss since it would be in addition to what the circumstances of war cause you daily, then I think that in that case you should not risk undertaking the next campaign, and you are authorized to conclude peace with the Ottoman Porte, even if the evacuation of Egypt has to be the principal condition. You must simply, if possible, delay the execution of that condition until the general peace.

You can appreciate as well as anyone, Citizen General, how important the possession of Egypt is for France. This Turkish Empire, which threatens to collapse on every side, is today breaking up, and the evacuation of Egypt by France would be the more unfortunate since in our time we should see this fine province in other European hands. What you hear of the success or reverses of the Republic in Europe must enter strongly into your calculations.

Accustomed to see the rewards for the work and hardships of life in the opinion of posterity, I am leaving Egypt with the greatest regret. It is only obedience, the interest and glory of our country and the extraordinary events that have occurred there that have determined me to go into the midst of the enemy squadrons to return to Europe. In heart and mind I shall be with you; your success will be as dear to me as if they were my own, and I shall regard as wasted all the days of my life in which I do not do something for the army I am leaving to your command and to consolidate the magnificent edifice whose foundations have just been laid.

All the soldiers of the army I confide to you are as my own children; at all times, even in the midst of their greatest hardships, I have had signs of their affection. Treat them with the same feeling; you owe it to the very special regard and friendship that I have for you and to the true affection that I feel for them. **(82)**

After the PROCLAMATION *to the Army of the East, the first of these documents,* CAPTAIN VERTRAY *describes the stupefaction with which the news of Bonaparte's escape to France was received.*

TO THE ARMY OF THE EAST. HQ Alexandria, 22 August 1799:

In view of the news from Europe I have decided to leave for France. I leave General Kléber in command of the Army.

The Army will soon have news of me; I can say no more. It is hard for me to leave the soldiers to whom I am most attached; but it be only for a time, and the new Commander-in-Chief has the confidence of the Government and of myself **(83)**

The news of the departure of Bonaparte produced a feeling of stupefaction in the ranks of the Army, but not despair. The prestige of the commander-in-chief had been greatly lowered during the campaign in Syria; it was generally thought that he despaired of firmly establishing French power in Egypt, and that we should also return to France. We all had great confidence in Kléber, who was much more considerate of the welfare of the soldiers, and more sparing of their lives than Bonaparte. But on the other hand there was great vexation amongst those attached to the fortunes of Bonaparte, and whom he just abandoned in Egypt . . . The campaign in Italy had made us enthusiastic, and the Army, which had become famous under the orders of Bonaparte, loved its commander-in-chief; but the expedition to Egypt had somewhat cooled our admiration. **(84)**

CHAPTER FIVE

THE SIEGE OF MALTA (1800)

After Bonaparte's return to France the British were confronted with the task of evicting the forces which he left behind him, that is to say the garrison at Malta under Vaubois and the army in Egypt under Kléber.

The blockade of Malta began after the Battle of the Nile, but it was not a task which suited Nelson's temperament and when he became involved in the affairs of the Kingdom of Naples and Sicily the duty fell to Captain Alexander Ball. Since both the Ottoman and the Russian empires were now in alliance as a result of Nelson's victory, a squadron appeared under the command of Admiral Ushakoff, but this was more concerned with the capture of Corfu than with assisting Russian allies.

Nelson's choice of Ball could not have been bettered. In theory, he represented the King of Naples, who claimed sovereignty over the island, but it was his encouragement of the Maltese levies which kept the siege going when no one else was interested in it. The popularity thus gained stood him in good stead when he became the first governor of the island.

Although it was obviously necessary to evict the French, neither Nelson nor the British government set much value on Malta, which, before the Suez Canal was built, had little strategic or economic value. On the other hand, it was vital that no other power acquired it. So at first an allied garrison was contemplated until it could be returned to the Knights of St John. But when neither Naples nor Russia made any effort to assist in the siege, and when the Tsar Paul changed sides to organise the Armed Neutrality of the North against Britain, it was proposed to occupy the island with British troops. After Paul's assassination in March 1801, it remained equally important to prevent his successor from becoming Grand Master. So, though the British undertook to leave the island under the terms of the Treaty of Amiens in 1802, they remained to counter the Russian threat and this was one of the causes of the renewal of war the next year.

The Siege Begins

When Nelson sent Captain Saumarez to demand the surrender of General Vaubois, he received this reply on 25 September 1798:
You have without doubt forgotten that Frenchmen are now at Malta. The future of its inhabitants is a matter which does not concern you.

With regard to your summons to surrender, Frenchmen do not understand such style. **(85)**

Nelson therefore sent Captain Ball with five ships, assisted by the Marquis of Niza in command of a Neapolitan squadron, to blockade the island, at the same time requesting information about the state of the place.
NELSON TO BALL *from HMS* Vanguard *at Naples, 4 October 1798:*
You are hereby required and directed to proceed in HMS *Alexander*, under your command, off the Island of Malta, taking with you the ships named in the margin, whose captains have my orders to follow your directions, and to use your best endeavours to blockade the Ports of that Island, so as to prevent any supplies getting in them for the French troops, as well as to prevent the escape of the French ships now in that place, delivering the dispatch you will receive herewith to the Marquis de Niza, who is cruising off that island.

Captain Murray, in HMS *Colossus*, has very handsomely offered his services to go for a few days with you off Malta, but will not interfere with the ships under your command. On meeting the *Incendiary* fireship, you will also take her under your command, he having my orders for that purpose. **(86)**

STATE OF THE ISLANDS OF MALTA AND GOZO ON THE 12th DAY OF OCTOBER 1798.
QUESTIONS

1. What force does the French consist of in the Islands of Malta?
2. What posts are they in possession of?
3. What quantity of provisions have they got and of what quality?
4. Are they sickly?
5. How near are the Maltese posts to those of the French, and what is the force and state of the Maltese opposed to them?
6. Have the Maltese any guns mounted, or any that can command the French posts or the ships in the harbour?
7. What is the number and state of the French ships of war in the harbour?
8. Have they any transports or merchant vessels ready for sea?
9. Of what description are they?
10. Have they any galleys or gunboats?
11. What are the Maltese most in want of?

ANSWERS

1. Supposed to be 3,000 soldiers and sailors, and not above 1,500 Maltese, of which not scarce 100 will take up arms for the French.
2. The whole city and all the posts immediately belonging to it, excepting Corradino, which is in possession of the Maltese, and commands part of the harbour. They have guns en masque, but not any works thrown up.
3. Corn for eighteen months, and mills plenty of oil, very little cheese; scarce the smallest taste of anything else. The acqueduct is cut off, but they have wells not likely to fail but in summer.
4. At the time of the insurrection there were 700 in hospital.
5. Corradino is very near the French posts. The Maltese are about 10,000 in arms, and could drive them out of several posts if of use, but the French could easily retire to St Elmo.
6. About twelve mounted: two on Corradino, four at Samrat, two or three at each of their camps. There

are thirty unmounted of different calibres.

No post of theirs commands any part of the harbour but Corradino.

7. Two ships of the Line and three frigates. The *Guillaume Tell* is much damaged, but may put to sea. The *St Giovanni*, formerly a Maltese 64, ready for sea; very old and in a bad state, and badly manned. *La Diane* and *La Justice*, French frigates in good order, and ready for sea. The *St Maria*, formerly a Maltese 40-gun frigate, badly manned, but ready for sea.

8. One cutter and four or five Greek or other merchant ships.

9. Only two of any size.

10. Two galleys and four gunboats.

11. Principally bombs and mortars. They also want more powder and muskets, and balls to fit their cannon, but cannot exactly tell their calibre. **(87)**

Bonaparte's victory in his Second Italian Campaign and the invasion of the southern states of Italy encouraged the garrison at Malta to hold out against the ill-equipped levies of the islanders.

NELSON TO ST VINCENT *from Palermo, 3 February 1799:*
My dear Lord, the *Incendiary* is just come from Ball, off Malta, and has brought me information that the attempt to storm the city of Valetta had failed, from (I am afraid I must call it) cowardice. They were over the first ditch, and retired, d--n them! But I trust the zeal, judgement and bravery of my friend Ball and his gallant party will overcome all difficulty. The cutter just going off prevents my being more particular. Ever your most faithful, NELSON.

P.S. Naples is declared a Republic, and the French flag flying. We are low in spirits, but all in this house love you. **(88)**

Ball was left to encourage the islanders and it is to his efforts that the acquisition of Malta is primarily due.

BALL TO NELSON *from HMS* Alexander, *off Malta, 9 February 1799:*
The inhabitants have deputed three gentlemen of good character to present a petition to His Sicilian Majesty and Your Lordship, praying that they may be put under the protection of Great Britain during the war, and unless it takes place I have every reason to assert that it will soon fall into the hands of another nation. I can perceive by Your Lordship's letter of the 25th of last month that you foresaw the necessity of this measure, and of the great check this will give to the disaffected Jacobins in the Island of Sicily. Your Lordship will hear from many quarters of the strong attachment which the Maltese evince for the English, whom they esteem from principle, and whom they fear, knowing we have always the means of punishing them, and they are now more sensible of it than ever, from their having experienced what they would not believe before, that a British squadron can block them up and starve them in the winter months . . . The Russians have not sent any proclamations here, and Your Lordship may depend upon my never allowing one of their ships to come in. Whenever any of them shall appear off the port I shall acquaint the commanders that the Russian plot formed last December in the Island, of which Guillaume Lorenzi was the chief, has occasioned the loss of a great many lives, which has so exasperated the Maltese that I could not answer for the safety of any of their ships.

With great deference I will venture to predict that Your Lordship is going to render your country a most essential service by annexing Malta to it, and it will give me an opportunity of proving your ideas, that by an economical government many islands would be a source of wealth to Great Britain. **(89)**

Doublet was now a Commissioner of the French army of occupation.

DOUBLET TO DIRECTORY *from Malta, 13 February 1799:*
With prudence and care for the inhabitants, with more precautions and surveillance, we may preserve this

28 Captain Alexander Ball from the portrait by Grimaldi

island in the state left by Bonaparte. Too sudden changes have caused the inhabitants to revolt and make common cause with our enemies.

Up to the present their attacks have not succeeded in doing more than destroying about a hundred houses in the town, to the east of the bridge, which used to be called La Sengle, Le Borgo and Bormola. The object of the English was to burn our ships and frigates as well as the arsenal and the magazine, which are in this part of the town, and which we can place elsewhere without great danger.

They are deceived in their hopes, but the garrison is extremely exhausted. The great heat and the bad food could produce disease and diminish the number of our soldiers. **(90)**

Nelson's poor opinion of Malta was shared by the Government—eg, Grenville to Dundas, 23 April 1800: 'In time of peace it is, I think, demonstrable that Malta would be of no use to us or France, for we both have direct access to all the ports and countries of the Mediterranean and want no emporium'.

NELSON TO SPENCER *from Palermo, 6 April 1799:*
My Dear Lord, I am happy that everything I have done respecting Malta has been exactly what has been wished at home. To say the truth, the possession of Malta by England would be an useless and enormous expense; yet any expense should be incurred rather than let it remain in the hands of the French. Therefore, as I did not trouble myself about the establishment of the Order of St John of Jerusalem at Malta, Sir William Hamilton has the assurance from his Sicilian Majesty that he will never cede the sovereignty of the island to any power, without the consent of his Britannic Majesty. The poor islanders have been so grievously oppressed by the Order that many times we have been pressed to accept the island for Great Britain; and I know if we had his Sicilian Majesty would have been contented. But, as I said before, I attach no value to it for us; but it is a place of such

consequence to the French that any expense ought to be incurred to drive them out. **(91)**

The Surrender
The strict blockade gradually wore down French resistance, but it was not for another year that they surrendered.

BALL TO NELSON *from HMS* Alexander *off Malta, 20 August 1799:*
My Lord . . . The Maltese armed peasants are so sickly that I ordered the Marines from the *Lion* and *Success* to be landed to strengthen the posts. I am informed that the French have not received the smallest supply of fresh provisions from this island or Gozo these last four months; they have eaten all the cats, dogs, horses and mules in the garrison. Mule's flesh sold for four shillings a pound a month ago, notwithstanding which General Vaubois keeps the garrison to their duty; his great object is to procrastinate until the blowing weather will enable his troops to embark on board the ships of war and make their escape. If your Lordship would come off here for a few days it might greatly accelerate the surrender of the garrison. The language of the French soldiers has been that they will oblige their general to surrender whenever a force appears off. I beg leave to suggest that if the English troops could be sent here from Messina with two 13in mortars a few battering cannon, powder etc., we could then carry on active operations and ensure a speedy surrender. **(92)**

General Abercromby, commander-in-chief in the Mediterranean, had sent Major-General Pigot to replace Brigadier Graham with 1,500 troops in the spring.

PIGOT TO GENERAL SIR RALPH ABERCROMBY *from Malta, 5 September 1800:*
Sir—I have great satisfaction in acquainting you with the surrender of the fortress of Valetta, with all its dependencies after sustaining a blockade of two years. The capitulation has been signed this day.

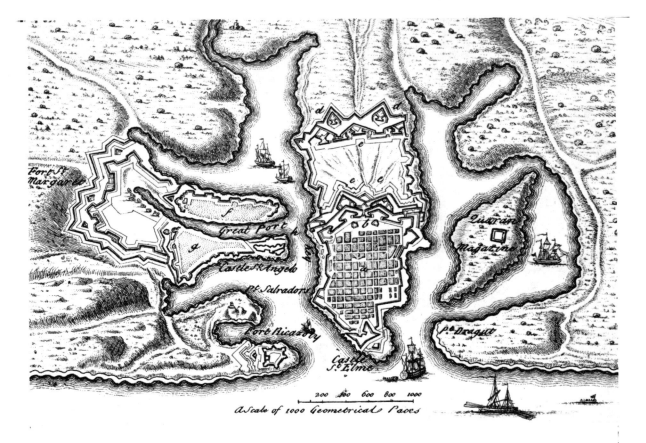

Labels on the map: Fort St. Margaret, Great Port, Castle Angelo, Pt. Salvadore, Fort Ricazoly, Casell S.º Elmo, Quaran Magazin, p.ª Dragut

200 400 600 800 1000
A Scale of 1000 Geometrical Paces

29 *A plan of the city of Valetta*

I had every reason to suppose that this most formidable fortress was likely soon to fall, from the circumstances of the two French frigates, *La Justice* and *La Diane*, going out of the harbour a few nights ago, one of which, *La Diane*, by the vigilance of the blockading squadron, was soon captured, and there are still some hopes that the other may have shared the same fate. Judging of how much consequence it may be that you should have the earliest intimation of this important capture, I have delayed until another opportunity sending returns of the stores etc., found in the place, which could not yet be made

up. In the short time you were here, you must have been sensible of the great exertions which Brig-Gen. Graham must have made with the limited force he had previous to my arrival with a reinforcement. He has ever since continued these exertions, and I consider that the surrender of the place has been accelerated by the decision of his conduct in preventing any more inhabitants from coming out a short time before I came here. He was sent to negotiate the terms of capitulation with General Vaubois, and I am much indebted to him for his assistance in that business.

I have great pleasure in acknowledging the constant and ready assistance and co-operation I have received from Captain Ball of HMS *Alexander*, who has been employed on shore during the greater part of the blockade. His name and services are already well known to His Majesty's Ministers, and I am sure I need not say more than that what he has performed here does credit to his former character.　　(93)

The poet S. T. Coleridge, having been secretary to Ball when the latter was Governor of Malta, wrote the following tribute to Sir Alexander in his periodical THE FRIEND:

The two men whom Lord Nelson especially honoured were Sir Thomas Troubridge and Sir Alexander Ball; and once, when they were both present, on some allusion to the loss of his arm, he replied 'Who shall dare to tell me that I want an arm when I have three right arms—this (putting forward his own) and Ball and Troubridge.

Never was greater discernment shown in the selection of a fit agent than when Sir Alexander Ball was stationed off the coast of Malta to intercept supplies destined for the French garrison, and to watch the movements of the French commanders, and those of the inhabitants who had been so basely betrayed into their power. Encouraged by the well-timed promises of the English captain, the Maltese rose through all their country towns and themselves commenced the work of emancipation by storming the citadel of Civita Vecchia, the ancient metropolis of Malta, and the central height of the island. Without discipline, without a military leader, and almost without arms, these brave peasants succeeded, and destroyed the French garrison by throwing them over the battlements into the trench of the citadel. In the course of this blockade, and of the tedious siege of Valetta, Sir Alexander Ball displayed all that strength of character, that variety and versatility of talent, and that sagacity, derived in part from habitual circumspection, but which, when the occasion demanded it, appeared intuitive and like an instinct. The citizens of Valetta were fond of relating their astonishment, and that of the French, at Captain Ball's ship wintering at anchor out of reach of the guns, in a depth of fathoms unexampled, on the assured impracticability of which the garrison had rested their main hopes of regular supplies . . .

Scarcely a day passed in which Sir Alexander Ball's patience, forbearance and inflexible constancy were not put to the severest trial. He had not only to remove the misunderstandings which arose between the Maltese and their allies, to settle the differences among the Maltese themselves and to organize their efforts: he was likewise engaged in the more difficult and unthankful task of counteracting the weariness, discontent, and despondency of his own countrymen —a task, however, which he accomplished by management and address, and an alternation of real firmness with apparent yielding. During many months he remained the only Englishman who did not think the siege hopeless and the object worthless.　　(94)

CHAPTER SIX

THE DEFEAT OF THE FRENCH ARMY (1801)

General Kléber had played a distinguished part in the Egyptian and Syrian campaigns, but he was known to be an opponent of the colonialist policy, having no faith in Bonaparte's dreams and little regard for the man himself. He was thus extremely angry when he found himself left in command of a demoralised army and a hostile, poverty-stricken province. He was determined at the first opportunity to take advantage of Bonaparte's reluctant authorisation that the evacuation might be negotiated.

In order to make contact with the Grand Vizir, whose army now lay on the frontier, he made Smith an intermediary. On 24 January 1800, the Convention of El Arish was signed on board Smith's ship between representatives of France and the Porte, its terms being ratified on 28 January.

Then followed an extraordinary diplomatic muddle which illustrates the difficulties of communications in days when it took two months to reach the Levant by sea. Knowing that something was afoot, the British government instructed Keith to inform Kléber that no armistice would be recognised unless the French army surrendered as prisoners of war. In ignorance of the fact that the convention allowing it to be transported back to France with the full honours of war was about to be signed, Keith brusquely informed Kléber of this policy in a letter dated 8 January, though it did not reach Cairo until 18 March. About the same time Kléber received orders from France that no capitulation was now permissible.

The convention being thus abrogated, the huge Turkish army advanced on Cairo, watched by an embarrassed Smith. Infuriated by what he naturally regarded as a breach of faith, Kléber defeated it at Heliopolis within sight of Cairo, which was also in a state of insurrection. Henceforward, a much tougher attitude was adopted towards its inhabitants. In his own words, Kléber was determined 'to squeeze Egypt as the lemonade maker squeezes the lemon'.

But on 14 June he was assassinated by a young Moslem fanatic.

The command now devolved, by seniority, on General Jacques Abdallah Menou, the leader of the colonialist party, who had been converted to Islam, much to the amusement of the army. 'As to our possession of Egypt', he informed Talleyrand, 'the Republic and the First Consul may rest assured that no power on earth can wrest that conquest from the Army of the East. If need be, we shall fight all the hordes of Asia and defeat them.'

Since experience had proved that the Turkish army was no match for the French, and being under the impression that the latter only numbered 13,000 men (in reality some 32,000) and that their morale was low, the British government decided in October 1800 to despatch an expeditionary force of 15,000 men to land at Aboukir Bay.

Sir Ralph Abercromby, an old and popular general, was put in command. Keith was told to provide transports and to make Smith his liaison with the Turkish fleet under the Captain Pasha. At the same time General Baird was ordered up the Red Sea from Bombay with 7,000 men. Having marched across the desert from Kosseir to Cairo and thence to Rosetta, they arrived a fortnight after all was over.

Both Abercromby and Keith were pessimistic about the prospect, especially after Major-General Sir John Moore had visited the Grand Vizir's army and pronounced it to be a rabble. However, an impressive armament of 140 ships assembled at Marmorice in Asia Minor opposite Rhodes. On 8 March 1801, a landing was made in Aboukir Bay against stiff opposition, Keith's flagship, the *Foudroyant*, actually fouling the wreck of *L'Orient* which Nelson had sunk nearly three years earlier. The organisation required to land 5,500 front-line troops in three waves of boats from transports lying far offshore, and the discipline required to gain a foothold on beaches well protected by artillery make the landing one of the most distinguished examples in the hazardous history of amphibious warfare.

At St Helena Napoleon told O'Meara, 'Had Kléber lived, your army in Egypt would have perished. Had that imbecile Menou attacked you on landing with 20,000 men, your army would have been a meal for them.' On 21 March, however, Menou fought a pitched battle, sometimes called the Battle of Canopus, to defend Alexandria. Casualties were heavy on both sides and Abercromby received a wound from which he died a few days later.

Sir Hely Hutchinson, an undistinguished general, now took command. Rosetta soon fell and the Turks reached Damietta. Leaving Coote to besiege Alexandria, Hutchinson took the rest of the army to attack Belliard at Cairo. The city capitulated on 27 June with the surrender of 13,000 men on terms identical with those of the Convention of El Arish eighteen months earlier. After a final battle, Alexandria was surrendered by Menou on 30 August on the same terms.

The day before the news was brought to London by Smith (who rode down Whitehall in full Turkish costume), the preliminaries of the Peace of Amiens were signed on 1 October, 1801. The presence of the French in Egypt had been the stumbling block to peace between Britain and France, although the other members of the Coalition had accepted the terms of the Peace of Lunéville a year earlier.

The significance of the Nile Campaign was much more than this temporary armistice. Not only did victory restore the prestige of the British army, not only did the discovery of ancient Egypt produce a new style of furniture and decoration, but Bonaparte had set in motion forces which destroyed the old order in the Middle East. When he invaded Egypt, western civilisation made its first impact in that area. The power of the Mamelukes was broken, the futility of the Sultan's power exposed, so that within a few years Mehemet Ali could begin to build a new and independent Egypt.

Convention of El Arish

CONVENTION FOR THE EVACUATION OF EGYPT, *agreed upon by Citizens Desaix, General of Division, and Poussielgue, Administrator-General of Finances, Plenipotentiaries of Commander-in-Chief Kleber; and their Excellencies Moustafa Raschid Effendi Testerdar and Moustafa Rassiche Effendi Riessul Knitab, Minister Plenipotentiaries of his Highness the Grand Vizir.*

The French army in Egypt, wishing to give proof of its desire to stop the effusion of blood, and to put an end to the unfortunate disagreements which have taken place between the French Republic and the Sublime Porte, consent to evacuate Egypt on the stipulations of the present Convention, hoping that this concession will pave the way for the general pacification of Europe.

1. The French army will retire with its arms, baggage and effects to Alexandria, Rosetta and Aboukir, there to be embarked and transported to France, both in its own vessels and in those which it will be necessary for the Sublime Porte to furnish it with; and in order that the aforesaid vessels may be more speedily prepared, it is agreed that a month after the ratification of the present Convention there shall be sent to the fort of Alexandria a commissary with fifty purses on the part of the Sublime Porte.

2. There shall be an armistice of three months in Egypt, reckoning from the time of the signature of the present Convention . . .

11. There shall be delivered to the French army, as well as on the part of the Sublime Porte as of the courts of its allies, that is to say of Russia and Great Britain, passports, safe conducts and convoys necessary to secure its safe return to France . . . Done, signed and sealed with our respective seals etc. January 24, 1800.   **(95)**

The circumstances and delays in communication which were responsible for the following letter are explained in the introduction. It is dated 8 January. The Convention was signed on 24 January. Keith's letter did not reach Kléber until 18 March. On receipt of it, according to a Turkish chronicler, he 'roared like an infuriated camel'. The Vizir's army was at the gates of Cairo, four times the size of Kléber's: nevertheless on 20 March he routed it at the Battle of Heliopolis, which is described below by Captain Vertray.

KEITH TO KLEBER *from aboard the* Queen Charlotte, *8 January 1800:*

Sir, Having received positive instructions from His Majesty's government not to consent on his Majesty's behalf to any capitulation with the French army serving under your command in Egypt and Syria, except on the condition of their giving up their arms, surrendering themselves as prisoners of war, and delivering up all the vessels and property of every description belonging to them in the port and city of Alexandria to the Allied Powers jointly; and in the event of such capitulation taking place, by no means to agree to the return of your troops to France until they have been regularly exchanged; I think it necessary to inform you thereof and to acquaint you that all vessels having French troops on board sailing from the country under the protection of papers signed by others than those lawfully authorised to grant them will be compelled by officers of H.M. ships under my command to return to Alexandria; but that all such as may be met with returning under protection of passes granted in consequence of a separate capitulation will be detained as Prizes and the people on board be considered as Prisoners of War. I have etc. KEITH.

(96)

KEITH TO ADMIRALTY *from the* Queen Charlotte *at Syracuse, 1 March 1800:*

Sir, I think it of the highest importance that their Lordships should be informed of the circumstances which have taken place in Egypt, and have therefore ordered Captain Maitland and Lt. Colonel Douglas of the Marine Corps to return to England, as they have been on the spot and will be able to give their Lordships what information may be wanting.

I beg to observe that the Convention has been made before Sir Sidney's receipt of Government orders on the subject; and although he does not appear to have signed it, nevertheless he has advised and consented thereto, and also has caused passports to be printed, to which his signature is affixed. These circumstances may in some degree change their Lordships' orders and determinations, as he has been the officer on the spot and may be considered as capable of granting terms to an enemy. Lord Elgin not only concurred but strongly recommended the measure. The Russian Ambassador has, by formal deed, consented to the terms.

General Douglas, whom I beg leave to mention to your Lordships as an officer of long and good service, seems to think that the army of the French in Egypt are so exasperated against General Bonaparte that their presence in France might be eventful.   **(97)**

The Battle of Heliopolis

CAPTAIN VERTRAY'S ACCOUNT:

The bad faith of England excited the indignation of the army. Kléber made known to the troops the terms of the capitulation which Admiral Keith had made to him and contented himself with adding the beautiful words: 'Soldiers! One only responds to such insults by victory. Prepare to fight!'

This short proclamation raised the spirits of everyone. Kléber ordered the Grand Vizir to return to Bilbeis on the frontier of Syria. The Vizir replied that he would never retreat. 'Diable!' said Kléber, 'I will force him to retreat tomorrow, and quicker than he wishes!'

The commander-in-chief assembled all the general officers at a council of war and explained to them his plan of campaign. The troops moved at midnight and took up their battle positions. On the right, General Friant's division: on the left, ours, commanded by General Reynier. The brigades formed in squares to the number of four, under the orders of Generals Belliard, Donzelet, Robin and Lagrange. The horse artillery occupied the intervals of the squares; the cavalry, commanded by General Le Clerc, was placed between the second and third squares. In rear, was posted the reserve.

The attacks of the Turks failed; our squares advanced and carried Matarick and Elanka. It was in this last place that we took some rest and refreshment. For twenty-four hours we had only one issue of brandy, made the night before the battle. The Turkish camp was luckily well provisioned and our men compensated themselves.   **(98)**

Three months after his victory, Kléber was assassinated. Captain Vertray describes the scene.

Kléber had gone to the palace where the headquarter offices were, which had been greatly damaged during the insurrection in Cairo. On the 25th Prairal (14 June), after holding a review, he came to the palace in the company of M. Protain, a member of the arts Commission, and they went to breakfast with General Damas, whose house was joined to the headquarters by a long terrace. The meal was a very gay one. Kléber was full of merriment and wit, and was much amused by some caricatures of the events taking place in France since the 18th Brumaire, drawn by General Damas, and about 2.0 p.m. he got up to return to the headquarters with M. Protain. Both quietly walked along the terrace, when a young man jumped out of a neighbouring reservoir, threw himself upon Kléber and struck him with a dagger in the left groin.

The General, staggering, propped himself against the parapet of the terrace and called a sentry—'Come to me, for I am wounded', and he fell bathed in the

blood flowing from his wound. M. Protain only had a cane in his hand; he struck several blows at the assassin's head, but the latter overthrew him, wounding him severely, and after having struck three fresh blows with the dagger on Kléber's body he took flight.

The murderer was a young native named Souliman-el-Alepi, aged 24 years, a writer by profession. As he refused to confess, they applied the bastinado to him on the soles of his feet, following the law of the country, but he persisted in his denials. Then the chief of the Mamelukes assured him that if he would declare the truth he would be set at liberty. He immediately confessed all the details of the crime . . . This young man was not a criminal by profession, but a fanatic whose religion had urged him to this horrible crime. A military court was nominated by General Menou to try the assassin and his three accomplices, the sheiks of El Hazar; these three were condemned to decapitation. Souliman, ran the sentence 'will have his hand burned, and will be impaled, then abandoned alive on the stake until the birds of prey have devoured his body' . . .

Menou, the new commander-in-chief of the army by right of seniority, was an officer without merit. He had been attached to the expedition by favour, and in Egypt he rendered no service of any account. His ambitions were satisfied neither by Bonaparte nor by Kléber, and Menou was jealous of the other generals. At Rosetta, where he commanded for two years, his intemperate habits made him the laughing stock of the army. One day in a mad fit he announced his resolution to accept the law of the Prophet and become a Moslem. This news provoked much mirth among us. The sheiks hastened to favour the conversion and dispensed with the disagreeable formality of circumcision. He took the name of Abd-Allah, Slave of God . . . These acts made him perfectly ridiculous in the eyes of the army and all the French residents in Egypt.   **(99)**

The British Expeditionary Force

The British government now decided that a force must be sent under General Abercromby to invade Egypt, while another one sailed from India under General Baird to attack from Suez.

SECRETARY FOR WAR TO ABERCROMBY, *Downing Street, 6 October 1800:*

From the intelligence lately received from Constantinople it is very much apprehended that the future efforts of the Ottoman Court will prove as ineffectual as those they have already made against the French in Egypt, and that there is considerable danger of the enemy acquiring a permanent footing in that country by interesting a part of the natives in their dominion and establishment, unless some powerful and immediate assistance is given to the Turks to cooperate with them in their expulsion. On the other hand, circumstances have recently transpired which leave little doubt that the present government of France will spare no sacrifices or exertions to send reinforcements to the army in Egypt, and that without some favourable change in the general state of affairs, or in the situation in Egypt, it would be found very difficult, if not altogether impracticable, to induce the French government by negotiations to relinquish its pretentions over that country . . .

Under these circumstances it is impossible not to look to Egypt as the point to which the greatest part of the disposable force under your command should be directed in preference to every other . . .

I have thought it right to direct a force of 4 to 5,000 men to be sent from India, to take possession of all ports and coasts of the Red Sea which are now occupied by the French Army. As this last mentioned force cannot reach its destination in less than four or five months, you will, in case of the French having previously agreed to evacuate the country, send the

31 *The British under Sir Ralph Abercromby and Admiral Lord Keith land at Aboukir in the face of a French force*

earliest intelligence of this event overland to Bombay, in order to prevent its departure; and in the contrary supposition you will endeavour to keep up a regular correspondence with the officer [Baird] commanding the detachment from India. **(100)**

The expeditionary force under Admiral Keith and General Abercromby left Asia Minor in company with a Turkish fleet. Keith describes the landing in Egypt in a DESPATCH TO THE ADMIRALTY *from Aboukir Bay, 10 March 1801:*

. . . Too much of the day of our arrival here had elapsed before all the ships could get to anchor to admit of the landing being effected before the approach of night; and an unfortunate succession of strong northerly gales, attended by a heavy swell, rendered it impossible to disembark before the 8th. The necessary preparations were made on the preceding night. The boats began to receive troops at two o'clock in the morning and at three the signal was made for their proceeding to the rendezvous near the *Mondovi*, anchored about a gunshot from the shore, where it had been determined they were to be assembled and properly arranged; but such was the extent of the anchorage occupied by so large a fleet, and so great the distance of many of them from any one given point, that it was not till nine that the signal could be made for the boats to advance towards the shore. The whole line began to move with great celerity towards the beach between the Castle of Aboukir and the entrance to the sea, under the direction of Hon. Captain Cochrane . . .

The enemy had not failed to avail himself of the unavoidable delays to which we had been exposed for strengthening the naturally difficult coast to which we were to approach. The whole garrison of Alexandria, said to amount to near 3,000 men, reinforced by many small detachments which had been observed to have advanced from the Rosetta branch, was appointed to its defence. Field pieces were placed on the most commanding heights and in the intervals of the numerous sandhills which cover the shore, all of which were lined with musketry, the beach on either wing being flanked by cannon and parties of cavalry held in readiness to advance.

The fire of the enemy was successively opened from their mortars and field pieces as the boats got within reach; and as they approached the shore the excessive discharge of grapeshot and of musketry from behind the sandhills seemed to threaten them with destruction, while the Castle of Aboukir, on the right flank, maintained a constant and harrassing discharge of large shot and shells; but the ardour of our officers and men was not to be damped. No moment of hesitation intervened. The beach was arrived at, a footing obtained, the troops advanced, and the enemy forced to relinquish all the advantageous positions which they held. The boats returned for the second division; and before the evening the whole Army was landed with such articles of provisions and stores as required immediate attention. I feel much satisfaction in conveying to their Lordships my full testimony of all the officers and men employed on this arduous occasion. KEITH. **(101)**

The Battle of Canopus

From the REMINISCENCES OF MIDSHIPMAN PARSONS, *who left Keith's flagship, the* Foudroyant, *to take part in the fight for Alexandria. The battle was named after the site of the ancient city of Canopus. It was particularly hard fought, Sir John Moore declaring that 'I never saw a field so strewed with dead', 1,040 French being killed and 240 British, among them General Abercromby.*

On the 20th March a Bedouin Arab sought Sir Sidney Smith in the British camp established before Alexandria. These Arabs (who are the robbers of the desert) came into the camp every morning thousands strong, forming a daily market of mutton, fowl,

32 Admiral Lord Keith from the portrait by Saunders

buffalo beef and vegetables, which, under excellent regulations, were sold at a very reasonable rate. Their appearance was wild and interesting and the son frequently led the ass that conveyed his blind father, numbers having lost their sight from the opthalmia, that dreadful scourge of the Egyptian shore. The Arab's information was important. He was sent by his chief to say that a large reinforcement of Frenchmen, with the commander-in-chief Menou, had been tracked and harassed by his band from Grand Cairo to Alexandria, into which place they had thrown themselves last night. On this important information, the order of the day commanded the assembling of the troops two hours before the usual time, which had hitherto been daylight.

On the following morning the men were mustering in the trenches and batteries when the vedettes rode in at a furious rate, their horses covered with foam. Their information convinced us of the discernment of Sir Sidney Smith in anticipating the measures of the foe. A numerous French army were advancing against us, stealing upon us in the darkness of the night. In came our advanced posts, who had been ordered to retire on the main body if overpowered. This was now that case, and they stated the advancing army to be in great force, and in a most excited state, from the quantity of brandy that must have been administered to them before they left Alexandria. Now the heavy and measured tread of the masses of infantry broke on the stilly silence of the night, while the neighing and prancing of the warhorse gave intimation of the cavalry being in great force on each flank of the advanced army. The stillness of death prevailed in our camp, save the dashing of the aides-de-camp in front of the line as they flew with orders from the general to the different batteries not to throw away their fire, but reserve the grape and canister till the enemy touched the muzzles of their guns. Our troops closed their files with bayonets glittering, which might be distinguished by the watch-fires that threw a lurid glare over our well-formed line, showing the firm determination of the troops by their compressed lips and the nervous grasp by which they held their muskets; their long and hard-drawn breath, the left foot slightly advanced, and the whole carriage betokening a firm determination to do or die, convinced the observing that their nerves were well braced to the deadly coming encounter. 'Silence, and steady, men', were the words of command heard along the line. The French trumpets sounded a charge, and everything was in wild confusion.

The British cheer rang high above the sharp volleys of musketry, the batteries threw in their death-dealing rounds, but the French army advanced in rapid style, overthrowing all before them, till the British bayonets transfixed their front rank; even that did not force them back. The survivors rushed on, and when day broke never were hostile armies more intermingled; here a Frenchman and there an Englishman. Now came the deadly strife of man to man; and the brave veteran who commanded in chief (he was upwards of sixty) was engaged hand to hand with a young French dragoon, and would have fallen under the weight of his sabre had not a friendly bayonet lifted the man out of his saddle, leaving his sword entangled in Sir Ralph's clothes. The gallant veteran seized the sword and shortly afterwards was shot close up to the hip joint by a musket ball lodging in the bone. The anguish must have been acute; but no symptoms, not even a groan, made known that he was suffering. When obliged to acknowledge himself wounded, he called it slight and refused to retire to the rear.

The Hon. Captain Proby, now addressing the commander-in-chief to whom he was naval aide-de-camp, reported the enemy to be retreating, covered by their cavalry. 'But good God, General, you are seriously wounded, your saddle is saturated with blood. Let me support you to the rear, and for all our sakes, let the surgeon examine you'.

'Captain Proby, I thank you', said the veteran in a faint voice; 'but in these stirring times the General should be the last person to think of himself. Captain Proby, order a forward movement and hang fiercely on to the retiring foe. Desire Hompesh's dragoons to cut through their rearguard and follow them closely to the walls of Alexandria' . . .

Sir Ralph, who was sinking fast from loss of blood, now turned to the manly form of his son, who stood at his side and muttered the words 'A flesh wound— a mere scratch!' and fell fainting into his arms.

He was quickly borne by orderly sergeants to the rear, where the wound was pronounced of a dangerous nature. Fortunately the *Foudroyant's* launch had just reached the beach to convey the wounded off to the shipping, and the hero of sixty-three, in an insensible state, was consigned to the care of his son, exposed to the fierce sun, whose rays shot down hot enough to melt him. Colonel Abercromby held one of his hands, while tender commiseration clouded his brow. I saw this gallant and good old warrior extended on a grating, coming alongside the flagship, his silvery hair streaming in the breeze that gently rippled the water—his venerable features convulsed with agony, while the sun darted fiercely on him its intense rays, combining with his wound to occasion the perspiration to pour down his forehead like heavy drops of rain; yet he commanded not only his groans but his sighs, lest they should add to the evident anguish depicted on Colonel Abercromby's countenance, as he wiped the perspiration from his father's face. **(102)**

The General died of his wound a few days after reaching the flagship.

As soon as the firing ceased, Sir Ralph was removed to the tent of Colonel Abercromby, where the wound was examined by a skilful surgeon of the Guards, who,

not finding the ball where he expected, advised that Sir Ralph should be carried on board a ship, to which he at once assented, and he was conveyed on board the *Foudroyant*, Lord Keith's flagship. Sir Ralph was placed on a bier and an officer who was present took a soldier's blanket and was adjusting it under his head, when Sir Ralph asked 'What is that you are placing under my head?' The officer replied that it was only a soldier's blanket; on which Sir Ralph said, 'Only a soldier's blanket! A soldier's blanket is of great consequence, and you must send me the name of the soldier to whom it belongs, that it may be returned to him'. **(103)**

The French Surrender

Menou promised to continue resistance in this LETTER TO BONAPARTE *from Alexandria on 29 May 1801, but the fleet under Ganteaume never reached Egypt or Ireland. The archaeological pieces mentioned passed into the hands of the British.*

I repeat, Citizen General, that we will perish, if necessary, to save the colony, but what has happened to our promised assistance? It is true that two vessels we have captured have declared that a Franco-Spanish force was in the Mediterranean. What has happened to it? English scouts have told our's that a French army has landed in Ireland.

I have sent back to Europe, as I had the honour of telling you, Citizen Consul, Generals Reynier and Damas, Inspector Daure and a few others. Most of the Members of the Institute and the Commission of Arts have asked to go too. I have thought it right to agree to their repeated demands. I believe they would have done better to await another opportunity.

I have kept the archaeological pieces, because, in the belief that we shall save the colony, I thought they were safer at Alexandria than on board a ship which might be captured. These objects are in a sacred depository.

Send help, General! In any event, the Republic

J. Atkinson del

R. Ackermann's Lithography 1st July 1817

At the battle of Alexandria a French Dragoon rode full at Sir R. Abercrombie and made a desperate thrust, though a good deal staggered by the shock the gallant veteran received his sword between his arm and side and in that manner so firmly grasped it that the Frenchman was compelled to abandon it.

and the Consuls can depend on the boundless loyalty of the Army of the East. ABDULLAH MENOU.

(104)

General Hutchinson, now in command of the British army, sent this final DESPATCH *to the Secretary of War.* This arduous and important service has at length been brought to a conclusion. The exertions of individuals have been splendid and meritorious. I regret that the bounds of a despatch will not allow me to specify the whole, or to mention the name of every person who had distinguished himself in the

34 *The wounding of General Abercromby*

public service. I have received the greatest support and assistance from the general officers of the army. The conduct of the troops of every description has been exemplary in the highest degree; there has been much to applaud, and nothing to reprehend; their order and regularity in the camp have been as conspicuous as their courage in the field. To the Quarter Master General, Lt. Col. Anstruther, I owe much for his unwearied industry and zeal in the public service, and for the aid, advice and cooperation which he has at all times afforded me. Brigadier General Lawson, who commanded the artillery, and Captain Brice, the chief engineer, have both great merit in their different departments. The local situation of Egypt presents obstacles of a most serious kind to military operations on an extended scale. The skill and perseverance of these two officers have overcome difficulties which at first sight have appeared almost insuperable.

During the course of the long service on which we have been engaged, Lord Keith has, at all times, given me the most able assistance and counsel. The labours and fatigues of the Navy have been continued and excessive—it has not been of one day of one week, but for months together. In the Bay of Aboukir, on the new inundation [before Alexandria], and on the Nile for 160 miles, they have been employed without intermission, and have submitted to many privations with a cheerfulness and patience highly creditable to them and advantageous to the public service.

Sir Sidney Smith had originally the command of the seamen who landed from the fleet; he continued on shore until after the capture of Rosetta, and returned on board the *Tigre* a short time before the appearance of Admiral Ganteaume on the coast. He was present in the three actions of the 8th, 13th and 10th of March, when he displayed that ardour of mind for the service of his country, and that noble intrepidity for which he has been ever so conspicuous . . .

Allow me to express my humble hope that the army in Egypt have gratified the warmest wishes and expectations of their country. To them everything is due, and to me nothing. It was my fate to succeed a man who created such a spirit, and established such a discipline amongst them that little has been left to me to perform, except to follow his maxims and to endeavour to imitate his conduct.

This despatch will be delivered to your Lordship by Colonel Abercromby, an officer of considerable ability and worthy of the great name which he bears. He will one day, I trust, emulate the virtue and talents of his never-to-be-sufficiently lamented father. **(105)**
By a firman *issued by the Porte in July, Lord Elgin's representatives at Athens (Lusieri and Hamilton) were granted permission 'to take away any piece of stone with old inscriptions or figures thereon' in gratitude for British help in expelling the French from Egypt. These were the Elgin Marbles now in the British Museum, which were shipped via Alexandria, though one of the three vessels was wrecked* en route *to Malta.*
ELGIN TO KEITH *from Constantinople, 9 September 1801:*

My dear Lord, I have written to Mr. Hamilton and in his absence to Col. Anstruther upon what savours of a job. It is this—I have been at monstrous expense at Athens where I at this moment possess advantages beyond belief. What I have secured is more valuable than anything that ever went to England, and I have more at my command. But this cannot be got without a large ship and English sailors, and the appearance of English colours. My most anxious wish therefore is that you would allow a large ship of war to go there for my purpose . . .

If grain is wanted, some is to be had at Athens, a good deal at Negropont. Now if you would allow a ship of war of size to convey the Commissary's ships and stop a couple of days at Athens to get away a most valuable piece of architecture at my disposal there, you could confer upon me the greatest obligation I could receive and do a very essential service to the Arts in England. Bonaparte has not got such a thing from all his thefts in Italy. Pray attend kindly to this, my Lord. Yours, ELGIN.

(106)
General Sir Henry Bunbury, a friend of Sir John Moore, explains the importance of the Nile Campaign in military history.

Thus ended the campaign of the British army in Egypt; a campaign of which the importance can hardly be exaggerated. Not only did the result remove the greatest difficulty in the way of peace, and dissipate the fear of England with regard to India, but the success which crowned our arms on the shores of Egypt had further consequences. It revived confidence and an honourable pride in our military service. The British nation, exulting in the proved valour and the triumph of their army, felt once more that they might rely on their officers and soldiers as securely as they had long relied upon their seamen. The high character of the British army shone brightly forth after the clouds which had hung heavily upon it. The miserable warfare in America, the capitulations of Saratoga and Yorktown, and the more recent disasters of our troops in Flanders and Holland, had fixed a deep distrust in the public mind of our military men. It was believed that our commanders, nay, even that our officers and soldiers, were degenerate and unequal to cope in battle with the conquerors of Italy and Germany. The trial which had now ended under great disadvantages first dispelled this prejudice. Our service regained its ancient standing in the estimates of the British people. Their confidence was confirmed, I trust irrevocably, by the great actions and victorious career of Wellington.

(107)

LIST OF SOURCES

1 *Letters and Documents of Napoleon*, translated by J. E. Howard (1961) No 258.
2 *A History of Malta* by W. Hardman (1909), 13.
3 Howard, No 283.
4 Dropmore Papers, Hist MSS Comm, vol IV, 193.
5 Howard, No 289.
6 Howard, No 291.
7 *Bonaparte in Egypt* by C. Herold (1963), 4.
8 Hardman, 44.
9 Howard, No 293.
10 Howard, No 197.
11 *Memoirs of Doublet* (1883) quot. Hardman 54, 60.
12 *Memoirs of Dolomieu* quot. La Jonquière, *L'Expedition en Egypte* (1899), I, 612.
13 *Memoirs of Bourrienne* (1836), I, 127.
14 Hardman, 48.
15 Howard, No 300.
16 Howard, No 301.
17 Hardman, 75.
18 *Spencer Papers*, ed W. H. Richmond (Navy Records Society, 1923) II, 437.
19 J. S. Tucker, *Memoirs of Earl St Vincent* (1844), I, 433.
20 Tucker, I, 437.
21 *Despatches and Letters of Lord Nelson*, ed Nicolas (1845), III, 20.
22 Nicolas, III, 17.
23 Nicolas, III, 30.
24 Nicolas, III, 37.
25 Nicolas, III, 40.
26 Nicolas, III, 45.
27 Nicolas, III, 42.
28 *Memoirs of Bourrienne*, I, 130, 160.
29 *Letters from the Army of General Bonaparte* (1798), 16.
30 Jonquière, II, 247.
31 *Authentic Narrative . . .* (Berry) (1798).
32 *Memoirs of Sir George Elliot* (privately printed 1863).
33 Nicolas, III, 53.
34 Nicolas, III, 55.
35 Nicolas, III, 61.
36 Nicolas, III, 56.
37 *Letters from Army . . .*, 206.
38 O. Warner, *Nelson's Battles* (1965), 82.
39 Bourrienne, I, 148, 153.
40 *Life and Adventures of J. Nicol* (1822).

41 Nicolas, III, 98.
42 Nicolas, III, 125.
43 Nicolas, III, 87.
44 Nicolas, III, 89.
45 Nicolas, III, 74.
46 Mahan, *Life of Nelson* (1897), 440.
47 Howard, No. 309.
48 Howard, No 311, cp Herold, 69.
49 Howard, No 320.
50 Howard, No 328.
51 M. Vertray, *The French Army in Egypt* (1899), 43.
52 *Letters from the Army . . .*, 76.
53 Howard, No 326.
54 Howard, No 329.
55 Bourrienne, I, 174.
56 Herold, 136.
57 *Letters from the Army . . .*, 140.
58 Howard, No 332.
59 Howard, No 353.
60 Howard, No 354.
61 Herold, 171.
62 Wallis Budge, *The Rosetta Stone.*
63 *Napoleon's Memoirs* quot. Herold, 183; cp De Chair, 151.
64 Herold, 190.
65 Howard, No 369.
66 Howard, No 380.
67 *Napoleon's Memoirs*, ed S. De Chair, 333.
68 Howard, No 382.
69 Herold, 210.
70 Vertray, 71.
71 Howard, No 388.
72 Jonquière, IV, 271.
73 Jonquière, IV, 284.
74 *Life of Sir S. Smith*, by J. Barrow (1848), I, 266.
75 Barrow, I, 276.
76 Herold, 300.
77 Barrow, I, 284.
78 Howard, No 398.
79 Howard, No 401.
80 Howard, No 402.
81 Barrow, I, 307.
82 Howard, No 411.
83 Howard, No 412.
84 Vertray, 100.
85 Hardman, 109.
86 Hardman, 132.
87 Nicolas, III, 156.
88 Nicolas, III, 254.
89 Hardman, 185.
90 Hardman, 181.
91 Nicolas, III, 315.
92 Hardman, 220.
93 Hardman, 323.
94 *The Friend* (1969 edn), I, 584, 554.
95 *Memoirs of Sir S. Smith*, by E. Howard (1839), I, 220.
96 *The Keith Papers*, ed, C. Lloyd (Navy Records Society, 1950), II, 205.
97 *Keith Papers*, II, 209.
98 Vertray, 106.
99 Vertray, 112.
100 *Keith Papers*, II, 242.
101 *Keith Papers*, II, 273.
102 *Nelsonian Reminiscences*, by G. S. Parson (1905), 85.
103 *Memoire of Sir Ralph Abercromby*, by Lord Dumfermline (1861), 199.
104 *Narrative of British Army in Egypt*, by R. T. Wilson (1803), 183.
105 Wilson, 181.
106 *Keith Papers*, II, 405.
107 *Narrative of Some Passages in the Great War*, by Sir Henry Bunbury (1927), 101.

ACKNOWLEDGEMENTS OF ILLUSTRATIONS